City of Panic

City of Panic

Paul Virilio

Translated by Julie Rose

Oxford • New York

This work is published with the support of the French Ministry of Culture – Centre
National du Livre.

ïi institut français

This book is supported by the French Ministry for Foreign Affairs as part of the
Burgess Programme headed for the French Embassy in London by the Institut
Français du Royaume-Uni

First published in France, 2004, by Editions Galilée
© Galilée, 2004, *Ville Panique*

English edition
First published in 2005 by
Berg
Editorial offices:
First Floor, Angel Court, 81 St Clements Street, Oxford OX4 1AW, UK
175 Fifth Avenue, New York, NY 10010, USA

Preface and English translation © Julie Rose 2005

Berg is the imprint of Oxford International Publishers Ltd.

Library of Congress Cataloging-in-Publication data
Virilio, Paul.
    [Ville panique. English]
    City of panic / Paul Virilio ; translated by Julie Rose.
       p. cm. — (Culture machine series)
    Includes index.
    ISBN 1-84520-224-4 (cloth)
    1. War on Terrorism, 2001- 2. Sociology, Urban. 3. Mass media—Social aspects.
4. Fear. I. Title. II. Series.

    HV6431.V57813 2005
    307.76—dc22

                           2005017025

British Library Cataloguing-in-Publication data
A catalogue record for this book is available from the British Library.

ISBN-13 978 1 84520 224 8 (Cloth)

ISBN-10 1 84520 224 4 (Cloth)

Typeset by JS Typesetting Limited, Porthcawl, Mid Glamorgan.
Printed in the United Kingdom by Biddles Ltd, King's Lynn.

www.bergpublishers.com

Contents

Foreword   ix

1   Tabula Rasa   1
2   The Democracy of Emotion   25
3   Kriegstrasse   47
4   An Accident in Time   63
5   City of Panic   85
6   The Twilight of Place   113

Index   145

To Heidi Paris and her work

Foreword

While I worked on this translation, the people of Beslan, North Ossetia, came out of their 'forty days in the wilderness' of mourning for the hundreds killed in the terrorist attack by Chechen rebels in September 2004; a further suicide bomb attack occurred in Indonesia, although the government of Indonesia finally charged militant cleric, Abu Bakar Bashir, spiritual leader of Jemaah Islamiah, with paternity for a prior act of terrorism; the memorial to those killed in the Bali bombings in October 2002 was unveiled at Kuta Beach; British worker Kenneth Bigley became the latest foreigner to be beheaded by terrorists in Iraq in full view of the world via the Internet; and yet another terrorist plot was dismantled in Madrid, the site of commuter train bombings ... where rescue workers were led to victims' bodies by the sound of their mobile phones ringing on unanswered through the rubble.

The 'X Prize' was won, as predicted, by the SpaceShipOne people, financed by Microsoft co-founder Paul Allen, and commercial civilian space travel is now as inevitable as today's commercial aviation became once Charles Lindbergh, aviation pioneer, anti-Semite and friend of Hitler, crossed the Atlantic without stopping in 1929, a feat the 'X Prize' aims to celebrate as an act of paternity.

George W. Bush's 'Global War on Terrorism' jumped the rails, and the bounds of strategic probity, in Iraq, where the 'Coalition of the willing' appeared to be losing the 'peace.' Meanwhile, the 'homeland,' any homeland, holds its breath, awaiting the attack from within. The world civil war Hannah Arendt thought we were heading for looks closer, from a certain perspective.

If that perspective and the current escalation of terror attacks seem to bear out the picture of gloom painted by *City of Panic*, Paul Virilio's sense of where the world is headed is radically different, though equally grim, in what is undoubtedly his blackest book to date. Written, necessarily, in the shadow of the World Trade Center attack, it extends that shadow backwards to the very conception of the modern metropolis in the radical notion that cities and civilian populations have been the target of terrorism for the past hundred years.

While insisting on the world's millennial mutations, specifically in the military order, as described in his groundbreaking essay of 1993, *Delirious New York*,[1] Virilio then relays that vision to the contemporary world-in-negative in which city-dwelling internauts morph into emotional and physical cripples, like *otaku*, those legions of adolescent Japanese computer nerds, living sequestered lives completely cut off from reality, and like cosmonauts insulated weightlessly in their capsules in a real or simulated void.

This insight is of a different order from any listing of global 'accidents' and incidents and that is the particular power of Virilio's diagnosis of the world's malaise. Joining all the dots, that diagnosis tells us that the acceleration and temporal compression of information technology and the mass media, and the political transmutations that follow, bringing us the 'democracy of emotion' and 'mass individualism,' cause us to lose our sense of reality; the world then closes in on itself, prior to being vacated.

I am aware of a small irony here. As I worked on the translation, I've been assisted hugely by Google and other search engines in tracking down recent comments and briefings, print media features and television news bulletins from which Virilio quotes in all his avid taking of the contemporary pulse. And though I was at times defeated by 'information overload' (or perhaps a certain arachnophobia in tackling search-engine 'spiders'), without such tools, I'd have been sunk because no bricks-and-mortar library in the world would have been to any avail.

Yet Virilio has never denied the usefulness of new technology. As he says, let others crow about the advantages; he is here to point out the downside, the shipwreck that is part and parcel of the ship... And the dangers are now so great, as Virilio identifies them, that the effervescent nerdspeak of a wired generation can seem as sinister as the loaded babble of genetic engineers. I myself have had the experience of living in a city under siege, as Hong Kong became under the SARS epidemic in 2003, with a whole populace disappearing behind face masks, avoiding human contact and shunning the very knobs and buttons, rails and surfaces of modern life. The experience demonstrated, among other things, that mass psychosis is lying under a very thin surface, one easily scratched.[2]

Since *City of Panic* was begun, other things have happened. Virilio, a Parisian born and (largely) bred, has left Paris and moved to the coast, to La Rochelle, Paris having finally become for him, not so much unliveable, as provincial: full of itself, arrogant, irrelevant. In La Rochelle, he has at long last gained the sea, 'la grand' rive'; his apartment looks out over the Atlantic, way past the fortress in the waves that Napoléon once built, to the ocean at large: to eternity. To misunderstand the pervading faith, particularly apparent in the final chapter, 'The Twilight of Place,' is to misread, or miss, the precise shade of black in *City of Panic*, a work in black not without issue.

I am reminded of the ultimate conversation of Shirley Hazzard's two lovers at the end of *The Transit of Venus*. Both, unknowingly, are about to die:

> 'Now they are speaking of telescopes of many metres, and of platforms in space.'
> 'It might be a way of discarding the earth, out of pique.'
> 'Because we couldn't make it work, you mean?'
> 'Because it was too good and great for us.'[3]

Notes

1. Virilio, P., 'Delirious New York' in *A Landscape of Events*, Cambridge MA and London: The MIT Press: 2000, translated by Julie Rose.
2. Rose, J., 'SARS and the City' in Davidson, C. *Log 1: Observations on Architecture and the Contemporary City*, New York Any Corporation, 2003.
3. Hazzard, S., *The Transit of Venus*, London: Virago, 2000 – first published in 1980.

1

Tabula Rasa

'Not to find one's way around a city does not mean much. But to lose one's way in a city, as one loses one's way in a forest, requires some schooling,' writes Walter Benjamin in regard to Berlin, well before the Situationists of Paris spiralled off into the blue...[1]

The education, in a way sentimental, of the passer-by who refuses to be a mere passer-by, begins extremely early, if not in childhood, when a child is under supervision, then at least in adolescence, that point when budding maturity is accompanied by the urgent need to cut loose, to escape.

Paris is the city I was born in and Nantes the city where I spent my adolescence. Paris meant 'peace,' the precarious peace of the 1930s, and Nantes, 'war,' total war. Between the two, I experienced exodus, the pilgrimage prompted by declared defeat, the journey of a population panic-stricken by the Fifth Column and fleeing under the shame of a sky invaded by the enemy.[2]

'The force of a country road differs depending on whether you are doing it on foot or flying over it in a plane. Only when you are travelling along the road can you learn something about its force,' Walter Benjamin goes on to say.[3]

This geodesic power is the power of the JOURNEY, the successive trajectories of a moving body oriented by its locomotive power, since there is no life except within the folds[4] – the folds of the terrain that protects or the pleats of a cadastral survey that violates our expectations. In fact, the space of the capital never has been whole but always fragmentary and increasingly fragile, whence its repeated riots, from the Middle Ages to May '68, via the Revolution and the Commune.

When, for example, I observe an aerial view of the Ile-de-France, I contemplate an unfamiliar agglomeration I've never clapped eyes on or set foot on before; and even if the map of Paris is not the same as the urban territory, such cartography is infinitely more precious to me than its view from the air, because it shows me the breaks, the fractures in the symmetry – in a word, the fractalization of a fabric that photography never lets you see.

Despite Haussmann, *Paris is not an open-air town.* The Baron merely bored a few visible axes straight across it as the crow flies, but he was not able to lastingly drill through the anonymous mass of *quartiers* beneath that *zinc envelope* that generations of roofers have thrown over Paris, like a shield warding off the gaze of the Medusa.

Here and now, down on the bitumen and a few forgotten cobblestones, are to be found not only those little islands we call 'arrondissements,' but grey areas, shadowy 'reserves of urbanity' – whence the originality of those *covered passageways* so beautifully analysed by that desparate runaway, Benjamin, as well as by Hugo, the insurgent of the sewers...

There again, NANTES completes PARIS, for the *Pommeraye* arcade, for me, melds into the passageways of the *Panoramas* along the *grands boulevards* of Paris. Following the lead of LYON, the Gallo-Roman capital full of *alleyways* known as *traboules,* Paris invented the 'métropolitain,' *a kind of traffic circuit habitable by means of carriages,* in which stations are so many semi-cylindrical public squares, sheltered from view as much as from inclement weather. If the Roman *insulae,* or islet, were just an immovable object, a piece of real estate, the metro tunnel is a pathway for the street furniture constituted by this underground network, which turns the capital into a marshalling yard in disguise.

Unlike the ring road known as the *périphérique,* that permanent 'state of siege' of the urgent stream of automobiles of the 1960s, the *métropolitain* is a public road network, a continuously rolling belt, which the mechanical pathways and stairs of its interchanges extend further for visitors to these railway catacombs, anticipating the transformation of the latter into air raid shelters in the 1940s...

But Paris is not all, PARIS IS NOT ALL PARIS. In 1936, when I was young, Paris meant Clichy in particular and its frequent popular demonstrations. It also meant the island of the 'Dog Cemetery' known as the 'isle aux chiens,' not far from la Grande-Jatte; and it meant Beaujon Hospital, my very first encounter with modern architecture. In 1937, it was also the Universal Exhibition and the discovery of an all-powerful technology, soon to become terrifying, in the historic showdown between the pavilion of Hitler's Germany and the pavilion of the Soviet Union.

I went from Paris to Nantes in 1940 and back again from Nantes to Paris in 1945. My return from exile took me back to Aubervilliers, beyond the fortifications of the 'Berlin Gate,' since renamed 'La Villette' no doubt in memory of the abattoirs that used to be there and that went by that name.

'What makes the very first view of a town or a village within a landscape so unrepeatable is that the far resonates in it in very strict communion with the near. Habituation has not yet done its work.'[5]

Conversely, when the discovery turns into habit, into habituation to the space of the different *quartiers* and we begin to find ourselves again, this clear vision fades, giving way to a blindness that favours automatic recognition of places.

To find or to rediscover? To know or to recognize? Between these terms, perceptive wholeness disappears, the city becomes an agglomeration, a sort of 'metacity,' a memorial of the paths taken by the passing object that I have suddenly become, I, the subject, this city dweller programmed by his motor functions every bit as much as by the road network system of the urban grid formed by all the different quartiers.

From that point on, the born Parisian becomes a receptacle, a *container*, of the national capital... My *ground capacity* is unbelievable: the orientation of squares and avenues is contained by my vitality, the city is present in the vividness of my memory of places.

Better than a mobile phone, I carry this 'mental map' everywhere I go. In the desert as in China, *my city is already there*, my domicile has become my domiciliation. Paris is more than accompanied baggage. *Paris is portable.*

Like an automatic recording device, my read–write head, capable as it is of reading existing data and accepting fresh input, has stored the routes, the return journeys.

From the Bois de Vincennes to Neuilly, from the Porte de la Villette to the Porte d'Orléans, where I currently reside, I've never stopped adding to my ATLAS.

What exodus achieved in my youth between Paris and Nantes, the chronic persistence of my alternating displacements has extended to the extreme limits of the world. From now on, foreign cities, like the *quartiers réservés* of my childhood, are no more than a long scrolling of preprogrammed sequences...

But this *capital to end all capitals,* this city-world, is the opposite of the City of Light as it presents itself in the dark clarity of the black sun of my memory, the imageless imagery of my mentality as a user.

Here, but where is that, in the end? Full sunlight means, exclusively, the great Orient of a directional organization, the fruit of my slow domestication. With no dusk and no dawn, the feeble luminosity of my mental imagery illuminates my steps more surely than any street lamp or this telesurveillance, which is only useful, in the end, to those privileged users that are the police.

If all the maps of Paris were suddenly banned – as maps were banned in Prague in 1968 – along with the names of the streets and the numbers on the buildings, I would still get around without any problem. Even destruction – TABULA RASA – would not be enough to throw me, as I was able to observe *de visu* in the centre of Nantes after the bombings of 1943, in Hamburg and Freiburg in 1953, and later on in Berlin... When it comes down to it, only reconstruction could really *disorient* me by demolishing the *constructions* of my memory.

Construction or reconstruction? Another question mark, another way of quizzing this *visual thinking* behind an appropriated milieu of which I am, so to speak, the unwitting and, especially, the unwilling architect – at least as far as any spontaneity goes.

Although I'd like to, I can't accept the overwhelmingly widespread belief in the culpability of the urbanists and architects involved in the drama of those *sensitive areas* of the Ile-de-France, without making this observation: *every city dweller is an unwitting urbanist.* In other words, an expert in the unity of time and place involved in movement from near to far.

Whence the endless sizing up on the part of users of the space of the different quartiers, users of the work of those achievers that are (often to our cost) engineers and architects.

Self-construction is therefore not, in this instance, some anarchic project as is the case with the favelas of Latin America. It is a common reality, predating every *construction*, which the vital needs of the ambulatory subject impose on each and every one of us.

In fact, since no vector can exist without direction, with the subject happily getting around town completely autonomously, the organization of routes imposes a self-construction of relationships that interferes with the one determined by the builders of the city. The programming of the road network of the urban terrain thus induces a position-finding system and mental appropriation in which *body* and *private world* start resonating, from nearest to farthest away.

Until now, the notion of self-construction was associated less with the vernacular architecture of the rural world than with the infamous shanty towns of contemporary metropolises. But construction and self-construction are actually intimately interconnected, not only within the inhabitant of the incriminated quartiers but equally within the architect whose profession we might see as 'superficial,' whereas his 'awareness of place' is native, similar in every way to that of his clients, the users of his buildings.

The extremely vehement criticism that is today levelled at builders who are now seen as directly responsible for the drama of the suburbs, has led to *systematic demolition* of the great residential estates of the Ile-de-France and is thus clearly a strictly suicidal feature of life in society.

Besides, the ritual festivities that preside over these acts of voluntary self-destruction, which include public concerts where the singing and dancing hordes applaud the putting to death of their former place of abode, clearly point to a return to collective terror, a terror that decapitates high-rise towers though not – not yet! – their authors, those culpable 'technocrat' builders of metropolitan modernity.

Responsible but not culpable, the offices of urbanism, and, conversely, *culpable but not responsible,* those who render unliveable (uncivil) these same quarters, *quartiers réservés,* reserved for demolition by implosion – only, a political implosion, streets ahead of the pyrotechnic implosion of the suburbs: those *faubourgs* that once saw the birth of Impressionism, however, at Argenteuil and Chatou, at Nogent and Suresnes, on the banks of the Seine…[6]

Now that we've taken this compulsory detour via the Paris ring road, let's go back to the centre of town, to the *métropolitain* tunnel, which is nothing less than the *crypt of the capital,* in order to look at an aborted but exemplary experiment in confusion regarding traffic circulation: I mean the installation at the exit of certain metro stations of *video terminals* aimed at replacing the old district maps.

Entitled *IN SITU,* the operating screen displayed perspective views of the surrounding *quartier,* with the possibility of zooming in using a long travelling shot, travelling all the way along the neighbouring streets.

This experiment of the RATP, like the experiment that put television in metro carriages, was rapidly abandoned and its spread suspended, despite the obvious value to advertisers of such visual displays outside the dark cinema hall that the underground network represents for metro users.

Telesurveillance of neighbouring streets only meant additional anxiety for harried travellers coming on top of the signal saturation of the railway labyrinth.

Indeed, when the traveller re-emerges onto the surface of Paris, he must once again rely on his sense of direction 'in the open' and, here – *HIC ET NUNC* – the image of the *IN SITU* network entered into conflict with the user's mental map: the *metro tunnel* could not morph into a *video tunnel* without immediately causing the 'passenger,' now once more a 'passer by,' to lose his spatio-temporal markers.

The 'space user,'[7] *could literally no longer find himself*, worse still, the filmed sequences telescoped the sequences produced by his customary motor functions... A bit more of the same and there would have been complete disorientation, vertigo! The real space of the user's visual sense could not bear the overloading of the virtual space of the metro's televisual signals any more than a motorist, blocked in the Paris gridlock, can bear to have to slow down as he drives across town. As one dismayed Parisian put it: 'It serves no purpose and it does your head in!'

In effect, the failure of the operation with the unfortunate name of IN SITU was a revelation of a general ignorance about the clandestine networks that irrigate Paris. As essential as water or the air we breath, streets are the corridors of the soul and the dark trajectories of memory.

Out in the open, the street is the mad dash of a race-pursuit as vital as the breath animating us... Describing the drama of the *faubourgs* of the nineteenth century, but also equally portending the drama of the great urban outskirts of the twentieth, Franz Mehring once wrote: 'I can't say how much the absence of streets depresses me.'[8]

The street, like the road which is an extension of it, is a horizontal precipice, scorched earth, a pediment open to every kind of assault. Whence the inherent difference between the antique *barricade* and the strike, the *general strike,* that momentary inertia which is merely a kind of despair of ever making progress...

In days gone by you used to obstruct the public thoroughfare to mark your opposition by practising 'clamour' – a collective howl signalling to the *seigneur* your discontent as subjects. But once trade unions and the press came on the scene, *it was a matter of creating a vacuum and keeping your mouth shut* before the eventual advent of the demonstration, the march from the Bastille to Nation or the other way round.

This explains the success of Baron Haussmann's strategy in increasing the number of bypasses, those great axes radiating outwards like spokes, to say nothing of the construction of the vast sewer network, the ancestor of the *métropolitain*. That brilliant show of hygienism was to lead the Prefect of Paris to aerate the capital by endowing it with squares essential for the repose of the masses, all the while launching parallel projects like the erecting of the Sainte-Anne asylum as well as the remand centre of la Santé, the ideologies of security and sanitation mutually reinforcing each other.

In 1868, in a celebrated pamphlet entitled, *Les Comptes fantastiques d'Haussmann*, Jules Ferry denounced the transformations of the capital that were down to Haussmann and that nonetheless had just dazzled visitors to the Universal Exhibition of 1867.

'You don't embellish, you demolish. You endebt, you crush the present and you compromise the future and it will be one of the enigmas of these times that your fantasies were able to last so long,' wrote the future Minister of Public Instruction.[9]

The enigma, the great enigma of history, is *the transport revolution*, which survives and transcends not only the Industrial Revolution, but the information revolution, with its highways, its peripheral feeders or sliproads, its proliferating underground networks, the RER and the METEOR, and the soon-to-be-completed third runway for the Paris region ... as though the construction of the *above-ground metro*, a hundred or so years ago, needed to double up, this time in altitude, with the *airlines* that saturate the skies of the Ile-de-France with their trails of exhaust.

Better informed about the bottlenecks of Paris than any number of experts, a taxi driver said to me one day: 'Listen mate, if the traffic's bad, it's because the streets are longer than they are wide,' thereby coming out not only on the side of Haussmann against Jules Ferry, but especially letting it be known that the Baron hadn't gone far enough in levelling the place with his roadworks... As though the future of the metropolis was not only the autodrome or the aerodrome, but a return to the desert, to TABULA RASA!

In effect, Paris is not all, PARIS IS NOT ALL PARIS. Paris is a long sequence-length shot, a tracking shot of over a thousand years that leads from Lutetia, centred in the Ile de la Cité, to the Ile-de-France, and tomorrow, or the day after, to this whopping great planetary suburb where the *metropolitics* of globalization will take over from the *geopolitics* of nations, just as the latter once took over from the city-state of the antique origins of *politics*.

In 1831, twenty years before Baron Haussmann, Victor Hugo wrote: 'They want to demolish Saint-

Germain-l'Auxerrois for some alignment of square or
street; in a little while, they'll pull down Notre-Dame
to enlarge the square out front; a few days after that,
they'll raze Paris to the ground to enlarge the plain
of the Sablons.'[10]

At the end of the day, Hugo was right: the advent
of the sky in History would bear out this expectation,
with the futurist innovations of Giulio Douhet in
the 1920s and, even more so, with the doctrine of
strategic bombing, which has subsequently turned
air strikes into a prelude for all wars, American or
otherwise.

After Dresden, and especially after Hiroshima
and Nagasaki, this 'aeropolitics' turned into a cosmo-
politics of nuclear terror, with the *Anti-City* strategy
that, until only a short while ago, still subtended
'the balance of terror' between East and West – in
anticipation of *GROUND ZERO* and the emergence
of an anonymous hyperterrorism capable of causing
the collapse not only of high-rise towers, but also of
this 'civil peace' between the peoples of a world in
disarray.

To illustrate this insanity, let's hear what Elsa
Triolet had to say on her return from Berlin: 'We
need to level everything, wipe the slate clean, tidy up,
disinfect and start again as if nothing had ever existed
over there. After all, the atomic bomb might have its
uses in such cases.'[11] Without knowing it, Aragon's

muse was reworking a phrase of Julius Caesar, who once declared: 'The greatest glory of the Empire is to turn its far-flung reaches into a vast desert.'

Yet note the slide operated between territorial antiquity and our aero-naval modernity, for the desert in question is no longer located at the far reaches – on the limes, the Roman borders. It is located *INTRA MUROS*, at the centre of the metropolis, as if the aerodrome now represented the impassable horizon, a negative horizon capable of cleaning up our political imperfections.

As the mayor of Philadelphia pointed out following the urban riots of the 1960s in the United States: 'From now on, a state's borders run inside its cities.' As a further proof of the 'air-orbital deterritorialization' under way in the age of globalization, look at the recent practice that consists of establishing a 'humanitarian protectorate' – in other words, temporary occupation – at the air bases of countries under such control, whether in Africa or Kosovo, with the American bases at Bondsteel, or today, in Iraq, in Baghdad or Mosul.

'When you speak of a great colony you are talking about a great naval force,' Michelet decreed, as you might recall. This phrase, while perfectly true of the age of *the ports of colonial trading posts,* must be brought up to speed today, for in the era of planetary globalization *airport bases* have taken over that role.

By way of example, note that the declaration of the cessation of hostilities in the second Gulf War was made on May 1, 2003 by President George W. Bush after he landed on the USS *Abraham Lincoln* off the coast of California. In terms of *negative horizons,* it might be useful to specify that, during this little media ceremonial, the ship's commander slowed progress towards the port of San Diego so that *the shoreline would not be visible in the background during filming.*

'The Earth is flat, it's only round at its extremities,' a comedian once joked. This assertion thumbed its nose at all relief, the relief of the mountains as well as of the hills that, according to geographer, Pierre Georges, form the thread of the history of France.[12] That thread lies buried beneath the density of metropolitan infrastructures that have, it would seem, freed man from the irregular surface of the ground: lifts, escalators of all descriptions, dirigible balloons, aeroplanes, helicopters, supersonic jets and stratospheric rockets ... all instruments of a progressive loss of the geopolitics of our origins in favour of a *metropolitics* that is fundamentally crepuscular.

As a result, urban activity has in fact been concentrated at the base of any natural relief available – to such an extent that the tower has gradually replaced the *hill* in such a way as to make ground floors uninhabitable sitting along avenues delivered up to the kinetic energy of transport in the manner of Shanghai, *where towers rise on podiums* at considerable height above the 'natural ground' and contain services, shops, leisure centres ... the whole kit and caboodle absolutely sealed off from the level zero of the city.

At the beginning of the 1960s, aviation chief, Brigadier General Chassin, declared: 'The fact that the Earth is round has not yet been taken into account by the military.'

Today, this geostrategic omission has been rectified with the belt of satellites looping around the Earth and the deregulation of intercontinental air transport, the very last 'hill' being *the rotundity of the Earth at its very last extremity!*

But let's return to our geographer's 'age of hills.' Why has relief become the stamp of the peopling of rural regions over the ages? Because the 'hill,' for the village, is the image of a 'limit,' the limit of a form of possession as well as of a form of protection – from the sunlit hills of Provence, ringed with terraces, to the west coast's mist-shrouded hills and the hills streaming with springs of the Morvan or the hills of the flat country of the north or the hills that poke up in Paris, such as Montmartre, Montparnasse or

Mont Valérien – *hills of war* today deserted in favour of their incessant overflight by the engines that take off endlessly from the 'air fields'...

Let's go back to the tower, to the 'skyscraper' that has defined American-style urbanization for over a century. A catastrophist before his time, Le Corbusier threw up his hands when confronted by New York: 'It's a cataclysm in slow motion!' He could not have known how right he was for, since September 11, 2001, the cataclysm has speeded up so fast that the very high building has become an impasse and the reconstruction of the World Trade Centre a *POSTMORTEM REVIVAL* of a skyline now as deserted as the *blue line of the Vosges* was in 1940.

Indeed, if the residential tower has replaced the hill, the Roman hill fort and the church tower, this is because it is the sole means of reaching the sky and stretching out vertically.

And now, with supersonic jets and rockets, *the tower has been motorized.* It has torn away from the ground and from gravity to shoot as high as it is possible to go, thereby acquiring the velocity needed to escape from terrestrial weightiness.

'Ultralight and motorized,' the very high build-ing has become mobile, shedding its architectonic density in order suddenly to become an 'arrow,' one not related to those of the gothic cathedrals or even of the Empire State Building, which was evacuated after the collapse of the Twin Towers just like the twin-tower building in Kuala Lumpur.

Since *GROUND ZERO* – and some forty years after the mayor of Philadelphia's declaration – the American state's borders are indeed running inside the metropolises of the twenty-first century, with their gangs, their militias and terrorists from whom no traditional war can deliver us. In Baghdad and Babylon, as in New York, the tower has definitely lost its architectonic supremacy, bowing down before all that takes off, all that flies over the world and its *geodesic* curvature, the final relief of the world's reality.

But let's get back to the Iraqi capital where, a short while ago, in the teeth of chaos, the coalition forces sealed themselves off behind concrete walls, the prize going in October 2003 to Paul Bremer's headquarters, this compound of five square kilometres now nestling behind walls three metres high and fifty centimetres thick.

Possessing total superiority in the air, the Anglo-American coalition has also benefited from *the 'Haussmannesque-Stalinesque' urbanization* of Baghdad, their armoured columns taking the wide avenues that cut through the fabric of the city in order to invade its centre.

Here again, note that the flatness of the highways and the international airport would have favoured the plan of attack designed by the vice director, J-3, operations of the Joint Chief of Staff. Major General Stanley McChrystal declared on March 25, 2003: 'We are going to lead a campaign based partly on KINETIC effects, partly on NON-KINETIC effects and partly on information-linked operations.'[13]

If the term 'partly' is certainly legitimate when you are talking about kinetic effects, when it comes to cinematic and media effects, by contrast, it is quite a euphemism, rather badly dissimulating the absolute supremacy of the GLOBAL INFORMATION DOMINANCE of the Pentagon.

From the beginnings of history, warriors have been keen to know 'what is on the other side of the hill.' Whence the construction of the *watch tower* that preceded the invention of the telescopic lens and was followed in time by television and 'forward scatter' telesurveillance of the very rotundity of the globe – what they call *the final hurdle.*

To achieve his aims, the watchman on the lookout has thus used every available means at his disposal, from the instrumentation of mountain summits whereby domination of the surroundings could be acquired DE VISU, to captive balloons and aviation as means of control at altitude prior to becoming means of transport, transporting death... Finally, we have stratospheric rockets and spy satellites.

But alongside these 'aero-' and 'astronautical' disciplines that convey the optical illusion of long-range vision, with television following hot on their heels, there was another less prestigious means of rising. I mean the hoist or freight elevator. Without that invention, deriving from the construction industry and public works, the tall building simply would not exist, for it is ultimately the *lift* that is responsible for the urbanization of the third metropolitan dimension.

In 1852, the American, Elisha Graves Otis, put together the first freight elevator, which was activated by steam, and presented it to the Universal Exhibition in London within the framework of the Crystal Palace. In New York, the same man would install the first *ELEVATOR* designed for passengers. *The express lift was born.* From a few metres a second at the beginning of the twentieth century, it was soon to acquire greater and greater speeds gaining thirty kilometres an hour, for instance, in the TWA Tower in New York, then forty-five kilometres an hour in Yokohama and eventually fifty to sixty km/h in the Millennium Tower in Tokyo, which would carry to an altitude of eight hundred metres 150 persons going nowhere in a hurry – except *high up!*

As I've written previously, the tower is a high altitude impasse. Yet the very latest promise of this *cul-de-sac* is currently being beefed up, with the recent invention project of the American, Dr Bradley Edwards, a researcher at Los Alamos. Edwards is racing to make headway with his innovation of the very first *orbital elevator*, which would involve setting up an offshore base station in the Pacific Ocean that would anchor a robotic platform boosted into space by means of a system of traction under tension using spools of carbon nanotubes (CNTs). The base station would thus hold the robotic platform in geosynchronous orbit 36,000 kilometres above the Earth's surface, the laws of gravitational attraction (apparently) allowing this – for want of acquiring *escape velocity* (28,000 km/h). The ultimate elevator would accordingly be able to save on the huge cost of launching the outer stage of rockets which is then lost or the use of space shuttles to put men and equipment into high earth orbit.

There is nothing more, it would seem, to say: between the flatness of the desert of the 'aerodrome' or the 'cosmodrome' and the extreme altitude of this TERMINAL TOWER – a mobile tower, like a desperate hyphen between earth and sky – the image of the horizon is buckling itself up.

'*The rope doesn't hang, the Earth pulls,*' as Victor Hugo judiciously specified. With this sudden 'Babelization' of the lift, we now have proof Hugo was right for what is to be feared here is not so much the fall of the angels, collapse, as the unending revolution of a circular disaster, analogous to the disaster of the effects of the centrifuge machine on apprentice cosmonauts!

In fact the world is not all, the Earth is not the universe, and the 'end of the world,' dreamed of by far too many fretful souls, is not an experiment but, more precisely, what the Anglo-Saxons call *a test.*

Notes

1. Benjamin, W., 'Berlin Childhood around 1900,' in *Walter Benjamin: Selected Writings* vol. 3, 1935–1938, Cambridge MA and London: The Belknap Press of Harvard University Press, 2002, p. 352.
2. Virilio, P., 'Urbain, trop urbain,' preface to *L'Insécurité du territoire*, Paris: Galilée, 1993.
3. Benjamin, *op. cit.*
4. Michaux, H., *La Vie dans les plis*, Paris: Gallimard, 1949/1972.
5. Benjamin, *op. cit.*
6. See Castro, R. and Denissof, S., *Impressionisme urbain*, Paris: Ecole Spéciale d'Architecture, 2000).
7. Perec, G., *Espèces d'espaces*, Paris: Galilée, 1974/2000.
8. Mehring, F. (ed.), 'Charles Dickens' in *Die Neue Zeit*, 1912.
9. Ferry, J., *Les Comptes fantastiques d'Haussmann*, Paris: Edition de La Villette, 2000.

10. Hugo, V., *Choses vues*, Paris: Gallimard, 2002, p. 71.
11. Aragon, L., *Oeuvres romanesques complètes*, vol. 3 Paris: Gallimard.
12. Georges, P., *Le Temps des collines*, La Table Ronde, 2003.
13. Major General Stanley McChrystal, cited in *Science et Vie*, May 2003.

2

The Democracy of Emotion

'Events wash over events, waves wash over waves, the fact floats on always, intact, without discontinuity, without change and without letup,' wrote Victor Hugo in 1842, regarding the accident that cost the Duc d'Orléans his life.[1]

In the age of media conformism, 160 years later, the standardization of opinion is at its peak and exemplariness has taken over from celebrity to the point where the expression 'to create an event' no longer corresponds to reality, a reality falsified by a multitude of props, audiovisual and otherwise.

To be exemplary now means *to create without any creation*, most often, in fact, by simple subtraction of the work. Whence the resounding success, in the course of the twentieth century, of the art scandal – as well as as the political assassination. Whence, also, the discreet discrediting of the celebrity of the *producer* (the craftsman, the worker…) from the beginning of the nineteenth century, as well as the *creator* (the artist, the poet…) over the course of the century that followed. And this only served to promote this 'angel of the banal' that has joined the angel of the bizarre celebrated by Edgar Allan Poe with the (media) success we're all familiar with, from *LOFT STORY* to *STAR ACADEMY*.

Today, when *all examples are followed* in real time by the hyperpowerful mass media, *an event is exclusively a break in continuity, an untimely accident,* that crops up and breaks up the monotony of a society in which *synchronization* of opinion cunningly finishes off the job of *standardization* of production.

'Being famous is horrible,' the actor, John Malkovich, recently lamented. Such a denunciation of contemporary celebrity in the age of globalization goes hand-in-glove with the threat that now menaces *copyright,* the sheer authenticity of a signature.

Now you can be dispossessed, by contract, of your own name once it has become a 'brand name' along the lines of what has happened to Inès de la Fressange or Yves Saint Laurent. All that now counts is the logotype and its promotional logomachy – the semantic argument behind it.

Note that this logic of contemporary MODELLING, of INTERNATIONAL INTEGRATION, which is suicidal in the long run for all true creation, also entails the overkill of the *accident for accident's sake,* that form of postmodern 'art for art's sake' that takes us from the *local accident* – of the kind involved in the *Challenger* space shuttle or the Concorde supersonic airplane – to the global accident involving ecology – of the Chernobyl kind. And this merely portends the fatal confusion between 'terrorist attack' and 'accident' – of the kind involved in the explosion at the fertilizer factory in Toulouse – uncertainty then becoming a feature of *the accident in knowledge* and no longer solely in the incriminated substance.

To create an accident rather than an event ... to snap the chain of causality that so perfectly characterises everyday reality, is a kind of *expressionism* now universally sought, as much by 'terrorists' as by 'artists' and all the contemporary *activists* of the age of planetary globalization.

Note also how, opposing this, a rather large number of literary and scientific bigwigs play on dissimulation,[2] or complete anonymity. I'm thinking of Henri Michaux in the past or Thomas Pynchon today, writers who refuse to grant any interviews whatsoever to the press and who systematically refuse to be photographed... Note also those 'sleeping' terrorists who have infiltrated daily life in all its banality and *who no longer even claim paternity for their acts* though they do manage, on the other hand, to spawn imitators, numberless epigones. We'll get back to them later.

When it comes down to it, there is a certain *pyromania* in *this thirst for exemplariness without real celebrity.*[3]

We were talking about creating an event... But isn't an accident an indirect kind of *œuvre,* a consequence of substance? The airliner *innovates* the crash on the ground or against the Twin Towers, every bit as much as lift-off from an airport... The ship or ocean liner *invents* its shipwreck at the same time as its launch. Since this is nothing short of obvious, why the feigned surprise in 1912 when the *Titanic,* the ocean liner that was unsinkable according to the advertising spiel of the White Star line, sank?

An accident is in fact an assault on the propriety of substance, an unveiling of its nakedness, of the poverty of *whatever, whoever is* confronted by *what happens* unexpectedly – to people as much as to their creations.

This is why this issue of the major event is so topical at the beginning of the twenty-first century. At a time when all-out mediatization is cobbling creation in all its forms, what remains of the notion of the *œuvre,* when the whole notion of the '*chef-d'œuvre*' has long since gone west along with the notion of apprenticeship? What remains of the parallel notion of the *author,* the *creator,* once God is dead, according to the equally promotional spiel of Frederick Nietzsche?

Today, when Karlheinz Stockhausen can say of Satan and the terrorist attack on the World Trade Center: 'It's the greatest work of art ever made,' he lends credence to the notion of a return of the tragic and also of the abandoned masterpiece, that *chef-d'œuvre* in negative, *by subtraction*, as we were saying earlier, which, like the accident, is only ever *a miracle in reverse* – in a word, a lay miracle.[4]

Proof, if proof were needed after Auschwitz and Hiroshima, of the birth of *philofolly* and of the aesthetics of disappearance that has marked the whole of the past century.

And so, the crisis in the 'work in clarity' and the return, the eternal return, of the *work in black,* [5] usher in the crisis in traditional and substantial celebrity based on actual production, on some concrete creation, promoting instead an exemplariness that is purely accidental. The terrorism of September 2001 is one of the ultimate manifestations of this – only, a panic-driven manifestation whose counterpart is the pathetic attack at Tampa.

It's worth recalling the circumstances of that anti-event. On January 5, 2002, Charles Bishop, a fifteen-year-old adolescent who cleaned tourist planes in exchange for a few flying lessons, took off without authorization from Tampa airport on board a Cessna 142.

Pursued in vain by two F15 fighter planes and a coastguard helicopter, Bishop flew with impunity over MacDill Air Force Base, which houses the US Air Force Central Command for Afghanistan, before ending his flight by crashing into the twenty-eighth floor of the Bank of America tower. On his body a letter would be found revealing that he subscribed to the tenets of Osama Bin Laden.

'He didn't really support Bin Laden,' according to Emerson, a friend of the apprentice kamikaze pilot of Tampa. 'He just wrote that to bignote himself. Maybe he only wanted to top himself so that he would be remembered.'

Pitiful pyromania! The suicide of a young kid puts in its place the 'martyrdom' of the kamikaze pilots of New York and Washington. As Hugo went on to say: 'The wisecracks that a misdemeanour gives rise to are much more alarming than the act itself. Nothing is more abhorrent than a crime that can't keep a straight face.'[6]

Miserable miracle of Tampa, where exemplariness struck once again and so much so that the press shot of the Cessna's tiny cabin, clinging desperately to the intact facade of the Bank of America, is, you have to admit, the perfect companion piece to the spectacular collapse of the Twin Towers.

Let's not forget that, if mimetism is characteristic of the conditioning power of the mass media, it is primarily a mark of childhood, of the childishness of 'art for art's sake' that, together with the rampant infantalism of advertising, is currently leading to the standardization of behaviour and, what is worse, to *the synchronization of emotion.*

Today, 'to create an event' means above all breaking with mimetism, with promotional modelling, the kind of propaganda that will shortly go cybernetic and which is, without a doubt, the most significant form of pollution we are faced with. And it is a form of pollution that is no longer ecological but ETHOLOGICAL, as well as mental, inevitably accompanying the globalization of social behaviour.

Whether we like it or not, to create an event now means *to provoke an accident.*

In a time in history when the PRESENT (the *live*) wins out hands down over both the PAST and the FUTURE, an event is no longer 'innocent.' It is guilty, guilty of either deviationism or revisionism vis-à-vis the singleminded thinking of the era of global modelling.

To create an event is thus to reject whatever is now nothing more than 'a thirdworlding of human societies,' representing a shift from the EXOCOLON-IZATION of erstwhile empires to the ENDOCOLON-IZATION of the terminal empire.

To create an event today is to revive a kind of thinking that is resistent to the cyber-mentality of

31

a reflex conditioned to this SYNCHRONIZATION of emotions of the information age that has come to finish off the job of the STANDARDIZATION of behaviours of the industrial age.[7]

'The main focus of the second Gulf War was not so much air strikes as the shock of images and ideas. While children and soldiers were getting themselves killed, television was transforming the war into a dreadful soap opera, with repeats and fresh episodes on the hour,' Jérôme Charyn wrote,[8] thereby defining the metamorphosis of a conflict in which weapons of *obstruction* (Saddam's bunkers) and weapons of *destruction* (missiles) yield their strategic primacy to these *weapons of mass communication* designed to strike people's minds... Or, to put it still more precisely, the *weapon of mass destruction* is subject to the weapon of a form of mass communication that overrides it in every way – the audiovisual impact (in real time) outstripping by a long shot, through its globe-spanning propagation velocity, the material impact, precisely targeted, of precision-guided explosive missiles.

It won't be too far down the track before a MINISTRY OF FEAR emerges that will, from the height of its satellites and satellite dishes, override the extremely outmoded MINISTRY OF WAR, with its armies in an advanced state of disintegration since the blossoming of a kind of hyperterrorism that no longer even requires the mass of armoured divisions because its weapons system is mainly constituted by the array of mass communication tools turned back on the enemy.

One proof among others of the disintegration of classic warfare is provided by the reversal of the number of victims, for in recent conflicts, losses are 80per cent civilian, whereas in the traditional war things were exactly the reverse. Once, an international war was clearly distinct from a civil war – the war of each against all. But now, every war remotely worthy of the name is firstly a WAR ON CIVILIANS!

Whence the possibility that the coming 'total war' will be nothing less than a WORLD CIVIL WAR rather than a local war and this metastasis will no longer affect nations and government institutions, but their populations, offered up to chaos in a holocaust.

We should point out at this juncture that, just like *matter*, war has three dimensions: mass, energy and information.

Every epoch of history has privileged one of these dimensions. M*ass* came first, with the mass of ramparts and armour, as well as the mass of the legions and divisions of armies on campaign.

Then came *energy*, the neuro-ballistic energy of catapults, bows and arrows and other siege machinery as a prelude to gunpowder and artillery, and then the energy of the motors of armoured engines and planes and finally, of the bomb and intercontinental missiles, vectors of delivery of the atomic weapon.

Today, it is the third – and in particular a fourth – dimension that carries the day with *information* and its instantaneous communication speed. Whence the sudden permutation in which the *INFOWAR* appears not only as a 'war of weaponry' but especially as a WAR ON THE REAL; a war entailing full-scale anni-hilation of the sense of reality in which the *weapon of mass communication* is strategically superior to the *weapon of mass destruction,* whether atomic, chemical or bacteriological...

And so, after 'war tactics' like camouflage and various lures capable of hoodwinking the enemy, the main strategem suddenly becomes *the speeding up of reality* creating a panic-induced movement that destroys our sense of orientation, in other words, our view of the world.

On his return from Beijing on April 26, 2003, the Prime Minister of France, Jean-Pierre Raffarin, remarked on the threat of the SARS epidemic: 'Psychosis is no way to govern.'

If such an assertion might be correct in peacetime, it is totally devoid of meaning in wartime and espe-cially in a terrorist and anti-terrorist war. If you need convincing, just listen to this recent statement by the

Israeli Transport Minister, Yossef Paritsky: *'We should not forget that we are fighting terrorists, not innocent civilians;* we are not at war with the Palestinian people but with terrorist organizations.'[9]

If such reminders are necessary these days, this is undoubtedly because there is a sickening risk that any war will lead to widespread civil war – not only in Israel and Palestine but in the whole of the Near and Middle East and, perhaps, beyond.

To dispel any doubts about this, let me quote Gazi Ahmed, a Palestinian Islamic fundamentalist intellectual: 'They kill our children, we kill their children. No place is safe any more, no civilians, no individuals are now spared. *It is open warfare – there are no limits, there are no taboos.*'[10]

What Ahmed is talking about here is a war without war aims! And indeed, with mass terrorism, the 'preventive war' is a war lost in advance. If you need convincing, all you have to do is look at the results on the ground of the last two such conflicts: 'Operation Peace in Galilee' unleashed by Tsahal in 1982 with the invasion of southern Lebanon and the siege of Beirut, or the disastrous consequences of the war in Iraq.

To continue the debate regarding the French Prime Minister's declaration, you could go so far as to say that *pyschosis is a terrorist way of governing which we have abused since the beginning of the twentieth century.*

In fact, the *individualist* nature of mass terrorism undermines the political form of war, which is official in nature, has limits and, more especially, has *actual war aims*.

With the levy en masse of suicide bombers and the accelerated psychological processing of legions of contingents of those called to commit suicide, the strategic structure of political conflict is collapsing. As Gazi Ahmed once again points out: 'When the Intifada started, Hamas had trouble recruiting a simple celibate to get themselves blown up in Israel. But now, students, fathers with children, poor people or people from the middle classes, candidates are lining up in droves to get in.'... To say nothing of women.

During this same tragic spring of the year 2003, Thomas Foley, a former president of the House of Representatives in America, actually went so far as to spell out that the term ROGUE STATE was scarcely a political concept, signalling in doing so that the notions of AXIS OF EVIL and AXIS OF PEACE, designed to stigmatize said *rogue states* or the opponents of the preventive war in Iraq, overstepped the boundaries of reasonable alliance norms and relations between nations.

North American Chairman in the America of the famous Trilateral Commission, Thomas Foley must have had even more serious misgivings about the purely emotional turn that was being taken, for example, with the 'trans-Atlantic crisis' centring on the difference of opinion over Iraq between Europe and the United States, for during a session of that august body in Seoul, he declared: 'When divergences between governments begin to be embraced by public opinion, there is an obvious danger of things getting completely out of hand.'[11]

The word 'danger' is not saying much when the issue here is one of the major hazards of the dawning twenty-first century and when the globalization of public opinion has recently taken an unexpected form, turning into a kind of DIRECT DEMOCRACY that is TRANSNATIONAL and, more to the point, TRANSPOLITICAL – just as fearsome for nation states as any dictatorship, whether of the markets or of some tyrant.

In the era of the all-out information war, is it possible to wage war against people's opinion for any length of time? The answer is no.

What we are faced with today is no longer the threat of a democracy of opinion that would replace the representative democracy of political parties. We are actually faced with the outrageous threat of a true DEMOCRACY OF EMOTION. And this means collective emotion, at once synchronized and globalized, the model for which could well be some kind of *postpolitical tele-evangelism*.

After the familiar havoc wreaked by the democracy of opinion and the delirious convulsions of politics-as-spectacle, one of the latest avatars of which is the election of Arnold Schwarzenegger to the post of governor of California, it is all too easy to imagine what damage this 'democracy of public emotion' could do, as it risks dissolving public opinion, as though by acid, promoting instead a kind of *instantaneous collectivist emotion* that populist preachers have been busily abusing every bit as much as sports commentators or rave party disc jockeys.

By continuing in this way, INTERNATIONALIZATION-MODELLING will lead fatally to the kind of political trance once staged by the scenographers of Nazism – at the Nuremberg stadium or the Berlin sports arena in 1943... This is to say nothing of the stadium shenanigans of the East – as far as Asia.

After the *ecstatic consumption* of brand-name goods, denounced by Noami Klein in her book *No Logo*,[12] the time (real time) of *ecstatic communication* will be upon us, and, as well, often enough, of an *hysterical commutation* whose secret the sectarian gurus have mastered; public opinion suddenly morphing into a kind of transpolitical emotion on the scale of this self-styled 'global civilization.'

If interactivity is to information what radio-activity is to energy, we are here faced with the extreme limit of political intelligence, because political

38

RE-PRESENTATION disappears in the instanteneity of communication, promoting pure and simple PRESENTATION.

After the long history of the standardization of public opinion in the age of the Industrial Revolution and its systems of identical reproduction, we are entering the age of the synchronization of collective emotion, with the Information Revolution no longer promoting the old bureaucratic collectivism of totalitarian regimes, but what we might paradoxically call *mass individualism*. The term is apt because each and every one of us, one by one, is subject to mass media conditioning in the very same instant. This is a mirror effect in which the televisual image becomes the privileged tool of the INTEROPERABILITY of physical reality, on the one hand, and of media-generated reality on the other. I have proposed to call this STEREO-REALITY.

Actually, what others currently term TELE-REALITY in no way fabricates the event as claimed. But it does contribute to multiplying it indefinitely – to the point of industrializing the exemplariness of what crops up, *ex abrupto*.

'When it comes to technologies, there is no right of soil or right of blood, but only the right of might,' David Nataf wrote in an essay with the revealing title, *La Guerre Informatique* (*The Data-Processing War*).[13]

I would add a qualification: we are not talking here about the law at work in regulating the 'law of the jungle'; we are talking about *the right of a takeover by force*, the media putsch, in which speed outclasses brute force, material force; and this speed is the speed of the light of electromagnetic waves without which the globalization of power would evaporate like a mirage.

Whence the new 'dictatorship of the short-term,' the TYRANNY OF REAL TIME, that is terrorizing the sole financial market as well as international political bodies.

Populism or tele-evangelism, the practices of audiovisual mind control seduce, it would seem, the anxious televiewer of the democratic deficit. As J.-P. Dubois explains:

> We are seeing a consumerist drift in which you treat yourself to an opinion the same way you select a detergent. You forget about the common good; on the contrary, it's every man for himself. You choose what suits you, in the immediate term. You thereby offer yourself the illusion of being a *coproducer*. This utopia is all of a piece with the one that subtends democratic systems as a whole.[14]

With the revolution in the private automobile, we were already familiar with the effects of DROMO-SCOPIC distortion created by acceleration of the vehicle's course, in the way the landscape traversed flashed past at great speed. Now, with the audiovisual communications revolution, we are seeing (*live*) disturbances in stroboscopic perception of information whirling past. Whence the confusion not only of our occular images, but especially of our mental images and so in that view of the 'objective world' that largely conditioned our various choices as well as the democratic representation of our parliaments.

Drawing on intelligence reports on the conflicts in Afghanistan and Iraq, George W. Bush declared, on April 13, 2003: 'Through a combination of imaginative strategies and the new powers of technology, we are redefining war on our terms.' Those few words, pronounced in the euphoria of victory, have the merit of hammering home for us the nature of the new American war: it is an *INFOWAR* that now aims *to damage the truth of the facts* and the reality of a world now apparently globalized.

Yet note that if *information*, that third dimension of armed combat, is at the same time *truth* and *reality*, it is also the ideal opportunity for an incomensurable lie, a lie that will soon constitute a major accident in the history of knowledge. By comparison, the 'negationism' of the recent past will turn out to have been a mere antiquated hint of what was to come.

In a certain sense, the 'information war' now appears for what it really is: no longer simply 'tragic' but 'satanic,' since it aims to annihilate the truth of a shared world.

On this level of polemical analysis, what Winston Churchill had to say when he was reminding us that in war, 'the lie is the first rampart of truth,' truly strikes us as a blast from the past: irrelevant.

The lie that is no longer tactical but strategic is no longer a weapon of obstruction able to protect *the true*. It is a weapon of mass destruction of the reality of the facts – something the aftermath of the war in Iraq amply demonstrates.

In 1947, after Hiroshima, Daniel Halévy purposely placed us within the perspective of an *acceleration of history*. Nearly sixty years on, we find ourselves within a *dromological* perspective, this time. This is the perspective of a sudden *acceleration of reality* in which our scientific discoveries are turning against us and where certain troubled souls are trying to provoke an *accident in the real* at any cost – meaning, this telescoping process that will make reality and fabricated truth indistinguishable. In other words, the complete arsenal of THE LOSS OF THE SENSE OF REALITY will be implemented.

Secret agent or agent of influence, director of military communications or *spin doctor*... The list of names is crying out to be expanded.

In 1980, before an open-air gathering of savants, John Paul II felt compelled to denounce the *militarization of science.* In other words, the militarization of knowledge... Since September 11, 2001, we have entered into the tunnel of a form of *militarization of information* for the *INFOWAR* has taken to absurd lengths the 'logistics of perception' that once favoured victory over the enemy through the acquisition of military objectives.

Today, ambition knows no bounds since it is now a matter of *smashing the mirror of the real* and thereby causing each and every one of us, whether allies or adversaries, to lose our perception of the *true* and the *false,* of the *just* and the *unjust,* the *real* and the *virtual,* in a fatal jumble of words and images that leads to the throwing up of this very last TOWER OF BABEL – which is supposed to achieve revenge, for America, for the collapse of the World Trade Center.

If we need confirmation of such iconoclastic delirium, look at what the INFOWAR, whose victims we have been, led the US Army to allow, without their putting up any kind of a defence and while the world stood and watched. I'm talking about the ransacking of the archeology museum – the National Museum of Iraq – and the library of Baghdad, a disaster that recalls the sack of the Summer Palace in China which was perpetrated by the Europeans and against which Victor Hugo himself rose up.[15]

And so, after the sacking of Mesopotamian memory and the pillaging of the treasures of Summer, this 'information war' revealed itself for what it was: *a war against history*, an attempt to destroy our origins.

A preventive war, not so much against this or that tyrant as against this 'immemorial' memory that just won't go away, or not fast enough for those who pretend to rule not the future, as formerly with 'the radiant future of totalitarianism,' but the present, the eternal *present* of the ubiquity and instanteneity of the real time of telecommunications.

'Fog leaves time as it finds it,' the saying goes... The fog of war, that particular fog, no longer even leaves us time.

Notes

1. Hugo, *op. cit.*, p. 135.
2. For instance, software programmers sworn to secrecy by contract and often protected by body-guards.
3. When huge fires raged around Sydney in 2002, more than half were thought to have been started, criminally, by very young pyromaniacs.
4. See Domenach, J.-M., *Le Retour du tragique*, Paris: Editions du Seuil, 1973.
5. Yourcenar, M., *L'Oeuvre au noir*, Paris: Gallimard, 1968.
6. Hugo, *op. cit.*

7. On April 18, 2002, Luigi Fasulo deliberately torpedoed the Piselli tower in Milan with his *Commander*-style plane. At the end of that same year, a motorized glider was diverted from its flight over Frankfurt by a Phantom 4 plane piloted by a psychology student who wanted to pay homage to the cosmonaut, Judith Resni, who disappeared in the explosion of the space shuttle, *Challenger*, in 1986.

8. Jérôme Charyn, 'Une enquête littéraire sur la guerre en Irak.'

9. Quoted by Allouche, J.-L., 'Raids israéliens sur Gaza: Tsahal au pied du mur,' in *Libération*, October 23, 2003.

10. Mari, J.-P., 'Voyage au cœur du Hamas,' in *Le Nouvel Observateur*, October 23, 2003.

11. Quoted by Pons, P., 'Japon et Corée redoutent l'imprévisibilité américaine,' in *Le Monde*, April 27, 2003.

12. Klein, N., *No Logo: Taking Aim at the Brand Bullies*, New York, London: Picador, 2000.

13. Nataf, D., *La Guerre informatique*, Paris: Presses de la Renaissance, 2003.

14. *Le Nouvel Observateur*, March 2, 2000.

15. See the beautiful book by Che Bing Chiu and G. Berthier, *Yuanming Yuan. Le jardin de la clarté parfaite*, Paris: Edition de l'Imprimeur, 2000, all about the Summer Palace.

3

Kriegstrasse

Towards the end of the 1930s, Paul Valéry noted: 'The sensivity of the moderns is in the process of wasting away, since we need more intense excitement, a greater expenditure of energy, for us to feel anything. This blunting of sensitivity is obvious enough in the general growing indifference to the ugliness and brutality of appearances.'[1]

Such indifference to horror, stemming from the First World War and soon to allow the abomination of the Second World War, at Auschwitz and elsewhere, took as its first name *Expressionism* and as its second, *Surrealism*. Surrealism was born of the atrocity of the real of which André Breton and cohorts were the (consenting) victims; in the end it favoured the amnesia claimed by both *moderns* and *postmoderns* at once... Since the end of the Cold War, this indifference has gone by the name of *terrorism*.

In this sense, and only in this sense, Karlheinz Stockhausen was right when he declared at the time that the terrorist scene in New York was, 'the great-est work of art ever made.' A declaration that, in my view, merits a correction, one made by a woman, Marguerite Duras, in the text and dialogue of the film, *Hiroshima mon amour.*

In both examples, the terrorist scene is first filmed then *put on a loop.* And that is the great novelty of the televised scoop of the terrorist attack on New York compared to the dropping of the atomic bomb on Nagasaki, which put an end to the Pacific war.

We should never forget the radiographic imprint of human bodies on the pavements of that irradiated city. They are a match, so to speak, for the bodies of the tortured in *Nuit et Brouillard,* another film of Alain Resnais.'

As for the much-vaunted NY 'art scene' centred around Marcel Duchamp and a handful of other refugees from Europe – that was never anything more than the labour of exile of those who averted their gaze from the Medusa of the twentieth century, deserting the fields of horror of totalitarianism.

The American writer, Saul Bellow, had this to say about this trans-Atlantic retreat: 'I have one reget that I might put very precisely: in all my novels, I avoided talking about the great events of the century. I never tried, even tentatively, to make room in my work for the feelings they gave rise to. *In that, yes, I disappoint myself profoundly.*'[2]

At the end of the day, such disappointment is surely symptomatic of a veritable 'avoidance strategy' of which art – so-called contemporary art and, in particular, the new American art scene – was cunningly able to profit, leaving pop culture to look 'revolutionary' and paving the way for Andy Warhol … to the detriment of the kernel of cultural resistance of a ravaged Old World…

Strange duplicity of a rearguard battle which claims to be avant-guard, with the panicky collaboration of those who fled Europe's shores at the very moment when the doors opened to the great slaughterhouses of extermination of the demolishers of History.

'Art is a game. Too bad for the person who turns it into a duty,' wrote Max Jacob.

To follow up those words of a man who was to disappear in the camp at Drancy in 1944, let us remember that traditional warfare used to be a 'military art,' with its theatre, its music and its sense of patriotic duty. Well now, the *theatre of operations*, this political stage where war was not pretty despite the splendid uniforms and the banners snapping in the wind created by cannonballs whistling past, has suddenly become a simple *screen*.

And it is no longer the smoke screen that used to mask the storm troops, but a *cathode screen*, that screen where the scopic impulse of terror is played out, replacing the ordnance maps and little flags pinned all along a front line that has today vanished.

Art and war? It is the same old story of representation, of forced and even fanatical heroization, from the dances of death of the primates to the great military parades of the Champs-Elysées.

The only thing that has changed with the recent advent of HYPERTERRORISM is the *synchronization of emotion,* a synchronization that cleverly completes the old government war propaganda and the *standardization* of opinions that psychologically extended the standardization of munitions, military supplies, what is now called the *interoperability* of weaponry – which gave rise, let's not forget, to the Industrial Revolution, with the necessary standardization of firearms and precise calibration of the barrels of guns and cannons.

Now, with the *Information Revolution,* calibration of public opinion and politically correct standardization no longer go far enough. They must be topped up with the *emotional synchronization* of the hordes, a process in which terror must be instantaneously felt by all, everywhere at once, here and there, on the scale of a global totalitarianism.

To calibrate the terror the average televiewer can tolerate, to play on time gaps, more or less lengthy intermissions between two major attacks, so as not to see public opinion swing the other way – these are so many media tactics and strategies indispensible to hyperterrorism in transforming the classic war into a veritable *arcade game,* more remote from the Battle of Stalingrad than from Star Wars.

And so, following the conquest of enemy territories, we are seeing the gradual conquest of the *mental images* of populations strung out by the *instrumental images* of televised terror, put into a loop on the scale of a perspective that has suddenly become planetary.

The *base of operations,* the *front line,* has suddenly been ousted by the *surface of the screen;* an INTERFACE whose occupation is now strategically essential to victory.

POINT, LINE, SURFACE are no longer missed once the VOLUME, the spatio-temporal amplitude of terror, is inflicted on each and every one of us in the same instant.

Once, with the conquest of the high points in a landscape's relief, the battlefield was above all a 'field of perception,' with its military vantage points and its topographic and ballistic horizons. Now it is the *field of perception* of globalization that becomes the no-ground of the mother of all battles. Whence the shifting nature and the now systematic looping of the sundry shattering events – accidents, terrorist attacks, disasters and cataclysms of all kinds – that are now plunging the whole of humanity into mourning.

By suddenly becoming (*live*) PRESENTATION, (classic) REPRESENTATION has thereby transmuted assault as we knew it, which involved a frontal attack by the enemy, into sheer *stupefaction of the masses.*

This effect of instantaneous mind control is now beyond the realm of the various expert commentaries to which the first Gulf War and the conflict in the Balkans accustomed us; it is also beyond the realm of the old-fashioned role of the spin doctors of a psychological war that has today been shunted aside by the anonymity of hyperterrorism.

The saying goes that 'hysteria is the enemy of Time.' If so, the real time of terror relayed in a loop is most definitely 'hysterical' and it is the time of globalization as a whole, whether economic, political or strategic. The time required for reflection has been outdone; the time of the conditioned reflex is the order of the day of grand terrorism.

'War is a simple art based entirely on execution,' Napoleon warned. In this context, the term 'execution' is to be taken in both senses: at once the putting to death of the adversary and as a short, imperative command.

But Napoleon's interpretation goes further, for we know that this genius of the war manœuvre who was to introduce on land a *total war* that only naval powers had until that moment practised, did not wish to leave any written traces. I am referring to the battle manuals that strategists have often so generously bequeathed, from Caesar's *War of the Gauls* to Marshall Rommel's *War Without Hate*, via Jomini's *Concise History of the Art of War*, which inspired the title of Cioran's *Concise History of Decomposition.*

For Bonaparte, having become the Emperor Napoleon, the surprise value of execution already took precedence over the memoir of action and so, apart from a few aphorisms, our hero maintained his silence knowing full well that, as his celebrated saying goes: 'to command is to speak to the eyes.'

All the 'postverbal' novelty of anonymous terrorism lies in this sudden perception of fright, this pyknoleptic 'small death' of free will, which is a sort of silent command as, with it, to intimate an order is exclusively to intimidate the onlooker's eyes and, now, everyone's eyes at the same instant, on a continental scale and no longer just the eyes of a troop of undisciplined soldiers, stunned into submission by their chief.

We should also realize that this form of *synchronic command* of collective emotion on the part of adepts of mass terrorism was inspired precisely by certain types of weapons used specifically against them, in particular during hostage-taking operations on commercial airlines. I'm referring to the stun grenades used to abruptly curtail the reaction of hijackers under attack by military commandos and to thereby avoid, as much as possible, any disastrous spraying of bullets around a cabin full of passengers.

Dazzling and deafening, this *audiovisual detonation* produces instant paralysis of the adversary without apparent injury. A bit like the Biblical weapon against the fugitives of Sodom and Gomorrha, it transforms its victims of the moment into pillars of salt.

Specialists in televisual manipulation ever since the terrorist attack of the Munich Olympic Games in 1972, terrorists have seized upon such manipulation as a perfect model for the *deflagration of collective perception* that was to come into its own later, in New York and Washington – weapons of mass destruction now applying themselves to world coverage of shattering events: natural disasters, industrial accidents and, finally, major symbolic terrorist attacks against the Pentagon and the Twin Towers, not only riveting the attention of millions of televiewers, but also paralysing the economic activity of the airline companies that, along with telecommunication tools, are *the sinews of war* in the era of globalization.

The hyperterrorists have thereby invented a new 'weapons system' in which the practical range of the local attack is greatly increased, rendered global, by the broadcasting power of that weapon of communication that the Internet and the many television channels together constitute. And so, at the dawn of the third millennium, hyperterrorists have launched a kind of instantaneous and aleatory war of which Clausewitz could have no inkling.

Indeed, with the projection of forces, from classic artillery to the more recent ballistic missiles, the destructive power of explosives has always been increased by the propulsive force of cannons or intercontinental rockets, the *weapon of mass destruction* proving to be equally a *weapon of communication* of such destruction.

Given this, we can more easily understand the extreme strategic interest, in the age of the future 'American Anti-Missile System,' of hacking into television circuits (CNN, Al-Jazeera...) as well as into the Web, that network of networks, a veritable 'cannon for shooting in corners,' bunker-busting every remotest nook and cranny of a planet now looping back on itself.

Speaking of the art of war, it is pretty hard not to go back in time to the *Quarrel of the Iconoclasts*. This is especially so, when what is annhilated is not only the OBJECT – the figures of the great Buddhas of Bamian or the Twin Towers – but also the image of the SUBJECT, and this, thanks to the very instantaneity of the TRAJECTORY, in other words, to the sudden telepresence of terror.

After the iconoclasm of metaphysical RE-PRESENTATIONS – pictorial, sculptural – an iconoclasm of physical PRESENTATION has emerged. And it is a terrorist iconoclasm that finishes off the auto-da-fé of texts with an 'audiovisual' auto-da-fé inflicted on the shared perception of a humanity gathered together in real time in front of its screens...

The *theology incarnate* of Christianity has thus been outstripped by the *theology disincarnate* of the suicide bombing, in which the crime against humanity presents itself in the eyes of all as the SUMMUM of the 'aesthetics of disappearance' that so profoundly marked the twentieth century, from the invention of the movie camera to Auschwitz and Hiroshima. This time it is the *ethics of disappearance* that have ravaged the world, a world where speed and morality have never ceased following diametrically opposed curves, from the blasting of the famous 'sound barrier' to the acquisition of 'escape velocity,' that panic-stricken symbol of a world in flight that portends the imminent coming of the catastrophe of CYBERNETIC nihilism, in which the synchronization of individual emotions will finish off the job of the standardization of public opinion, which will then be unanimous.

At this level of interpretation of the secret relationship between art and terror, the so-called 'crisis in contemporary art' is no more than an epiphenomenon. Indeed, how can that little mindgame, art, long survive the *monopoly of emotions?*

In other words, how can art survive the lack of any game within a draconian form of conditioning? How can it survive this duty no longer of memory but of violence that makes the 'politically correct' a deadly prelude to the *optically correct*, that is, to a *Weltanschauung* that will outdo all the academicisms and all the conformisms of the past...

And so, following the *sacred art* of the origins of culture and the *profane art* of a modernity that touted itself as democratic, we are now seeing the emergence of an *art profaned* by this iconoclastic terror that paves the way for nihilism, since the 'creator' disappears along with his work in mass suicide terrorism, the self-mutilation of a social body that takes the sadistic rituals of the Viennese Actionism of the 1960s to their logical extreme. And it does so on the arrogant pretext of some MARTYROLOGY (Islamic funda-mentalist or otherwise) for, as we all know, if holy witnesses, religious martyrs, once preferred death to life cut off from faith, today's martyrs incite mass murder in the name of a faith that has become a verit-able *duty to depopulate the world.*

Let's hand over to a forgotten humanist, Albert Schweitzer, at this point: 'The enemy is, like anyone else, a host of the mind.'

But that was yesterday, or the day before – in days that now seem remote. With the mass suicide bombing, this hospitality on the part of the other altogether disappears, sent packing by the duty to do violence as part of the military anarchy that recently kicked off the third millennium.

'Immediacy is the order of the day for the print media,' they often say. What they don't say, though, is that immediacy is also on the menu for any mark or written form and so, also, for the so-called contemporary 'visual arts' that are contemporary with a world in crisis – in other words, with this *hysterical globalization* that has recently brought about the economic shipwreck we are all familiar with.

An art that registers or tends to register, along with all market forces, exclusively within the worldwide time of trade, is no longer a CONTEMPORARY ART but an ATEMPORARY art whose perspective is no longer temporal – historic – but timeless and geographic.

For want of any *temporal depth*, or in other words an historical perspective, this LIVE ART enlists solely like any other merchandise in the financial dromosphere of the globalization of the art market – anticipating the coming crash of its basic value, which will shortly extend the collapse in value of the new technologies of the image (digital or otherwise), those famous new technologies of information and communication start-ups, or NTIC, which recently took a battering on the stockmarket with the collapse in telecommunications prices.

On this subject, let's hear it from one of the high priests of Progress, Al Gore, former Vice-President of the United States and one of the people principally responsible for the launch of 'information superhighways': 'Uncommon power has combined with uncommon greed to create immense deceptions and losses.'[3]

You could hardly hope to put it better... But those deceptions and those losses do not implicate multinationals and their virtual speculations alone; they also concern the whole of cultural and artistic SOCIO-DIVERSITY, now threatened with extinction following the example of the great threat gnawing away at the BIODIVERSITY of all species of flora and fauna.

So, whether we like it or not, art is now part of the TERRORIST SCENE. And unless we come to terms with this tragic fact, we cannot make sense of the 'crisis in contemporary art,' the extravagance of a so-called 'freedom of expression' that is no longer anything more than the *freeing up of the terror attack* not only on *propriety* but on *value*, on all the ethical or aesthetic values that, until now, gave the *art scene* its significance.

Here, the propaganda perpetrated by the over-hyped *Rape of the Crowd*[4] is itself outdone, rendered

obsolete for the same reasons as advertising, that 'art'
that has inspired the visual arts since Magritte all the
way down to Warhol and co., with 'capitalist realism'
succeeding socialist realism before disappearing in
turn into the current ART BRUT of immediacy, that
panic-driven tele-reality that prolongs the customary
obscurity.

And so, with the emergence of the *accidental war* of
mass terrorism, in September 2001, the political art
of the *substantial war* becomes once more an ART OF
TERROR; the old army headquarters then makes way
for the 'Ministry of Fear,' for a kind of panic inflicted
on the whole world, the cathode screen standing in
for the 'frontline' of the old 'battlefield' of a war
once officially declared as such in days gone by.

This explains the relatively recent principle of
transpolitical blurring between the terrorist attack
and the accident, the fatal confusion between the
operation of destabilization in a state of civil peacetime and the attack of an anonymous enemy whose
furtiveness no longer allows the act of acknowledgement of declared hostility.

Hermann Broch might be allowed to have the last
word here: 'A world that blows itself up won't let us
paint its portrait anymore.'[5]

Notes

1. Valéry, P., *Cahiers 1894–1914*, vol. 2, Paris: Gallimard, 1988.
2. Interview with Fritz Raddatz, translated from the German and reprinted in *Le Nouvel Observateur*, March 7, 2002.
3. Gore, A., 'Broken promises and Political Deception,' in *New York Times*, August 4, 2002.
4. Tchakhotine, S., *Le Viol des foules par la propagande politique*, Paris: Gallimard, 1939.
5. Broch, H., *Création littéraire et connaissance*, Paris: Gallimard, 1966, p. 254, preface by Hannah Arendt.

4

The Accident in Time

International integration, globalization: the third millennium is confronted by the geophysical limits of the only habitable planet in the solar system. HUMANS born of the humus, in other words, of MOTHER EARTH, we are above all EARTHLINGS, inhabitants of an ecosystem without parallel in the Milky Way.

How are we going to approach the impending *incarceration brought on by Progress* without lapsing into despair over this finiteness that contemporary globalization portends?

To be more precise: finiteness does not mean the end of the world, the Apocalypse. It means that an apple is only an apple, a man is only a man and the Earth is only land.

Now, the thing is, with globalization, what we are experiencing today is the finiteness of the world, of a planet confronted by its ultimate exterior, the void of outer space. Whence the sudden foreclosure of a world that is globally finished, confronted by its 'extermination,' that is, by the perfect rotundity of its terrestrial substance.

'Completion is a limit,' Aristotle cautioned in his second axiom. In the twenty-first century, humanity as a whole is faced accordingly with its landed finiteness and with the related danger of also having to come to grips with its *human finiteness*: a kind of exclusion that is not only social and political but also physical, with the imminent explosion of a third bomb in the wake of the atomic bomb and the information bomb. I mean the genetic bomb, a bomb already presenting transgenic engineering as a symptom.

FORECLOSURE, EXCLUSION. You can't have one without the other in this geophysical incarceration contemporary with the acceleration of reality and not just of history now. Whence this latest shore, the ultimate skyline, not of the real-space perspective of the Quattrocentro any more, but of this VERTICAL LITTORAL constituted by the separation between cosmic emptiness and geophysical fullness.

FULLNESS, FINITENESS of the human environment: in order to better understand this situation or, if you prefer, this 'inventory,' we might, for instance, look at the recent *Living Planet Report* provided by the World Wide Fund for Nature in 2002.

According to the WWF study, our *biological footprint*, which is an estimate of the minimum productive surface required for a group to satisfy its needs in terms of resource consumption and waste disposal, already amply exceeds Earth's capacities in certain countries. To put it in slightly different terms, if everyone in the world lived like the average Frenchman, we would need more than two planets and if everyone consumed what the average American consumes, we would need five.[1]

But that is just the purely ecological aspect of the issue, for the biological footprint in question in the report speaks to us solely of the 'productive surface,' meaning space, and not of this space-time involved in the acceleration of technological Progress that reduces the extent, the fullness of the world to nothing. In other words, the eschatalogical aspect of our problem has been left out. Which explains the already old-hat emphasis on the illusion of the conquest of space by astronautics.

There was actually no real conquest of space in the twentieth century. There was only a conquest of 'transit time' by means of the excessive speed of those engines that attained, then exceeded, the *escape velocity* required to be freed of Earth's gravity which is 28,000 kilometres per hour. As for *habitable space*, this is limited to the self-contained celestial body we call Earth and to pressurized space capsules and sundry self-contained spacesuits worn by astronauts on board such capsules.

On board, but for how long? The recent accident of *Columbia,* following hot on the heels of the *Challenger* accident, would seem to lend support to those who have been hoping for the end of manned space flights and for the alternative development of robotic probes as a priority precisely to palliate the insurmountable *temporal problems* of the excessively long durations involved in remote missions.

In the end, beyond the blue planet, there is only the *conquest of emptiness* through acceleration of the sundry vectors of astronautics. Sure, we can traverse outer space, but we can't stay anywhere on the surface of those sterile stars that surround us on all sides... A female astronaut at NASA put it fairly vividly: 'How many light years away is the next waterhole?' It is true that when it comes to amniotic fluid, women have a certain edge.

But let's get back to the different signs of INCAR-CERATION.

For some time already, certain astronomers have been jumping up and down about the major natural hazard posed by ASTEROIDS. The last to hit us goes back to June 30, 1908 when a comet or asteroid – nobody knows which – exploded over Central Siberia at Tunguska. It was such a massive explosion that it caused extensive damage over more than 2,000 square kilometres of tundra.[2]

Recently named NEAR-EARTH ASTEROIDS or CRUISERS, these menacing celestial objects are beginning to spawn vast detection programs – all American, note – such as LINEAR, or Lincoln Near Earth Asteroid Research project, the most impressive of them all, employing two automated telescopes, equipped with electro-optical detectors, previously used by the military for *detecting Soviet satellites*.[3] Reconverted at the end of the Cold War, these instruments have since been affected to the search for errant asteroids.

However, as the system incorporates a large *blind spot* that does not allow it to observe the Southern Hemisphere, rigging out that half of the world has become a matter of great urgency, according to François Colas, of the Institut de mécanique céleste of the Paris Observatory.

Strangely, this system of cosmic defence, which joins the ANTI-MISSILE SHIELD of 'Star Wars,' relaunched in 2001 by President George W. Bush, appears as history's *ultimate rampart*, after the fortified walls thrown up around towns or the Great Wall of China, to say nothing of the Maginot Line or the Berlin Wall.

Another clinical sign of the GREAT HEMMING IN is the exponential development of *GATED COMMUNITIES* and the return to the walled city, notably in the United States, where several tens of millions of Americans have been locking themselves away for the last ten years in quest of the ultimate comfort, INTERNAL SECURITY.

Private cities, protected by their electronic fences, surveillance cameras and guards, one of these ghettos is even called *FORTRESS AMERICA*... Those on the subcontinent, such as the five ALPHAVILLES that now ring Sao Paulo in Brazil, don't bear mentioning.[4]

These are all so many symptoms of the pathological regression of the City in which the *cosmopolis,* the open city of the past, gives way to this *claustropolis* where foreclosure is intensified by exclusion of that stray, the outsider, what we might call a SOCIOCRUISER, who is threatening the metropolitan inhabitant's peace of mind the same way the stray NEAR-EARTH CRUISER is threatening the terrestrial environment only to shortly require us to erect an EXOSPHERICAL fence to fend off the dangers of the void.

At this juncture we might point to a strange coincidence between the advent of the CHAMBER OF WONDERS 400 years ago and the emergence of the CHAMBER OF CATASTROPHES.

The chamber of wonders crops up in the sixteenth century in *a world that was opening up* thanks to maritime conquest,[5] which brought with it the discovery of exoticism in all its forms, notably with the *cabinet of curios* of the seventeenth century.[6] But the coming opening of the ACCIDENT MUSEUM is contemporary with a world that *is closing in on itself* only to occupy itself, in the twenty-first century, with ecological endotism, in expectation of the first stirrings of a kind of eschatology that democracy will one day have to deal with if it wants to avoid disappearing under the threat of a new tyranny, the TYRANNY OF REAL TIME, this 'accident in Time' belonging to an instanteneity that is the fruit of a technological progress out of political control.

'…an inconceivable life of stress, of power, of endeavour, of unbelief – the strong life of white men, which rolls on irresistible and hard on the edge of outer darkness,' wrote Joseph Conrad on the subject of modern man.[7]

At the threshold of the third millennium, it is not only the whites but the whole of humanity that is camped on the edge of outer darkness, on the razor's edge of the emptiness of outer space, hoping against hope for some ultimate colonization, not over the seas, now, but OUT OF THIS WORLD.

If the city is the most important political form of history, then the world-city that is contemporary with the age of planetary globalization does, indeed, have its back to the wall. And that wall is now the wall of time – 'the time barrier'; this real and astronomical time that has now outpaced the time of calendars and the ephemeris.

This, as we have seen, explains the emergency return of the 'walled city' and of the BUNKERIZATION that is blighting cities everywhere, bit by bit. It also explains the anti-missile shield of the United States and the anti-asteroid belt against cruiser asteroids hurtling towards us from deep space...

If *completion is a limit*, that limit is to be fortified these days against all intrusion, and this, on the scale of a geographical metropolis located here or there, wherever, as well as on the scale of the only habitable planet in the solar system.

We are thus, right now, ineluctably faced with the sudden revelation of a CRITICAL SPACE resulting from temporal compression, the telluric contraction of the space-time of the interactive activities of humanity in the age of a globalization that is at once economic, political and military.

Whence the crucial issue of the reversal of the notions of INSIDE and OUTSIDE which is merely the topological consequence of the crisis in dimensions: dimensions at once geometric and geographic.

Such consequences are 'catastrophic' in the sense meant by the late lamented René Thom. Today they mark the decline in the GEOPOLITICS of nations to the benefit of an administrative METROPOLITICS that restricts the way urban spaces are populated.

At the very start of the wars of the state of Israel, one of the Knesset deputies was driven to deliver a prophecy: 'Israel is too small for peace!' He thereby defined the future of Israeli-Palestinian conflicts, but also the return to the endemic disease of wars between cities that marked the distant epoque of the city-state, which preceded the nation-state.

So there is no reason to be surprised at the imperialist nature of this 'mobile warfare' that was to take over from 'siege warfare'... Siege warfare that we have gone back to in the age of globalization with the reappearance of the 'private city' surrounded by fences and surveillance cameras. The 'great metropolitan retreat' of the twentieth and twenty-first centuries actually reproduces, but on a global scale, what used to happen once upon a time on a local scale with the population movements of the agrarian and artisanal age.

After the Industrial Revolution and, more particularly, the revolution in transport and transmission, this tendency has not only overwhelmed towns and cities, with their nebulous peripheries but, equally, nations and continents, now converted into 'fortresses' (Europe). Whence the generalized BLITZKRIEG that has, little by little, replaced mobile warfare and large-scale territorial invasion, with, as sole horizon, the *polar inertia* of a completion or, more precisely, of a FINITENESS that is now eschatological and not merely ecological.[8]

71

'Adventure, as it now presents itself to us, seems to me vasty different from adventure as we once knew it, which had more to do with geography than with humanity... This extraordinary new form of adventure is now driving Europe and the World. *The geographic jigsaw puzzle has been pulled apart and quickly slips into new images that will replace the already shattered images of the old worlds,*' wrote Pierre Mac Orlan in 1950.[9]

Well before the emergence of fractal geometry, the poet of the 'social gothic' divined the fracture that was about to happen in a world apparently 'whole' but that would soon be gasping in labour, producing the contractions with which we are all familiar.

At the *relative speed* of the transport and movement of bodies and goods: territorial conquest of the expanse of the *real space* of geophysics.

At the *absolute speed* of the transmission of the messages of interactivity: conquest of the lack of expanse of the instanteneity of *real time*.

Whence the sudden pathological clamping shut of a once multipolar world that has now decided to go *unipolar* with the reversal of the notions of *inside* and *outside*.

As I tried to explain ten years ago or more:

For the military planners of the United States, the GLOBAL means the *inside* of a finite world and the LOCAL means the *outside*, the outskirts or periphery.

And so, for the US Army, the pips are no longer inside the apple any more than the segments are inside the orange; the skin has turned inside out since orbital ASTROSTRATEGY turns GEOSTRATEGY inside out like a glove! The world's exterior is no longer the surface of the Earth. It is everything that is *in situ*, precisely localised here or there.

So there you have it, the very latest globalitarian mutation: a mutation that extraverts locality, every locality! This time the expatriation is global, affecting the fundamentally 'geopolitical' identity of nations as well as of human societies as a whole.[10]

'All countries are tempted to let multilateral diplomacy slide when it comes to what is happening in their own backyards. The problem is that the backyard of the American superpower is the same size as the world.' This observation on the part of the Assistant Secretary-General of the UN is indicative of the topolgical reversal of erstwhile imperialist geopolitics.

The metageophysical contraction of the space-time of the finite world thus has as an ultimate consequence – with the irremediable loss of expanse – the FORECLOSURE of the dominant power's field of action.

And so, from now on without distance and without delay, *a state of emergency is becoming widespread.* This is one of the little understood aspects of the accident integral to the political economy. Whence the revealing line of a student in Durham, North Carolina: 'We can't wait to be attacked before we strike back. Those days are over and it's time the planet realized.'

This peculiarly panic-riddled statement is characteristic of the *offensive* aspect of the temporal compression of the world in the age of globalization and so, of the fatal setting up of the *preventive war* as a means of control on the part of the last empire.

We can't wait any longer since the lack of waiting time strips us of the sovereignty that was conferred upon us, in the past, by the immensity of continents. In other words, *the whole world has become too small for peace*, this civil peace between nations and their respective populations now threatened by a never-ending *state of emergency* – that other figure in the 'state of siege' that is, this time, planetary.[11]

'The Earth really does look like a ball rolling down a sharp incline with its speed increasing as it rolls according to familiar laws.' Pierre Mac Orlan was already offering this helpful hint at the beginning of the 1930s, that decade of such sinister memory. Similarly, today, eschatology determines human ecology and will soon even determine politics.

As in the days of Nazi *Lebensraum*, space is no longer only VITAL. It has suddenly become TERMINAL and *we need to act everywhere without delay* so as not to be caught napping.

Whence the topological reversal evoked earlier, in which the GLOBAL means the interior of the finite world and the LOCAL, its exterior... In other words, all that is still *IN SITU*, precisely located in a geophysical space where the importance of distances has disappeared in the face of operational interactivity. And so, with the instantaneous globalization of real time, we find ourselves once more faced with a veritable foreclosure of the political field where erstwhile territorial sovereignty no longer rates.

But when it comes to the failing sovereignty of 'failed states' – a concept, we should note, that the Pentagon is trying hard to get off the ground in order to justify its right of intervention – what we really need to realize is that this 'failure' affects America as the hyperpower just as much as anyone else, forced as it is itself to anticipate its own interventions according to the strategy of the preventive war. And this is a clinical symptom of the weakness of the supreme power faced with the rise of chaos resulting from the closing in of the world.

This, among other things, is what the ACCIDENT INTEGRAL to political reality comes down to, the much-touted 'failure' of *rogue states* spreading everywhere and involving not only weak, destitute countries but the strong ones every bit as much, in a world that is, as we were saying, debarred.

An obvious fact flows from this acknowledgement of bankruptcy and it is that Euclidian geometry no longer in any way fits the geography of human power!

Geopolitics and geostrategy are both wiped out in turn, along with the internal borders that once separated states and their respective civilizations.

We are thus entering the TRANSPOLITICAL age where everything is globally EXTERNAL since the internal, the INSIDE, is the ultimate limit, the FINITENESS of the world, and the external, its FULLNESS.

In other words, *everything that takes place*, here or there, above as below, in the East as in the West, has suddenly been hit with exclusion, because of the fact of foreclosure *hic et nunc* of our history.

Having reached this point, we can confirm, without too much risk of getting it wrong, that the era of political REVOLUTIONS is over and that we are now entering, under duress, the disturbing strangeness of the age of transpolitical REVELATIONS.

In the middle of last century, Pierre Mac Orlan went on to write:

The end of the world should tidy up a number of doubts. You might suspect such an end of being at the mercy of man's unlimited power, or, what would be more consoling, of some ordinary toss of the dice, in a game our cosmogonies simply haven't worked out yet. It must be said in defence of humanity that no political party so far has had the bright idea of listing the end of the world in its program.[12]

That particular oversight is now being made up for with the emergence of ecological politics on the one hand and, on the other, the accelerated globalization that has seen the spectre of a third anthropological type shoot into prominence. After the predator and the producer, meet the *exterminator*, freed from all restraint.

In a recent article on Iraq, Jim Harrison declared: 'We have triggered this war with satanic idiocy. Many Americans think we are living outside history.' Much more realistic than first appears, this claim is still not quite complete, since the current 'American megalomania' is not only outside history, but outside the geography of *the finite world* Paul Valéry glimpsed, in this *OUTLAND* that has taken over not only from the *HINTERLAND* but also from the *NO MAN'S LAND*... In other words, within this globality that is outside everything and now claims to be the centre of a world gone OMNIPOLITAN.

This world turned inside out like a glove by the speed of temporal data compression suddenly reverses the poles Pascal spoke about, because the circumference is now everywhere and the centre, nowhere.

Wherever the local empire once depended on cities, the global empire comes up with a monopoly or, more precisely, an excentric megapoly that is never anything more than the achievement, this time definitive, of what the Ancient Greeks called SYNECISM.

Indeed, in Hellenic Antiquity, the POLIS, which was to give politics its very name, was initially a sort of telluric phenomenon and therefore fundamentally geopolitical, since scattered villages joined together beyond their ethnic particularities *to form a city...* A state-city, a city-state.

Now, at the very start of the third millennium, the ultimate synecism is no longer so much geophysical as 'metageophysical,' given that the grouping of an agrarian population has been superceded by the OMNIPOLITAN concentration of these *visible cities* on the road to advanced metropoliticization, which are slated to soon form the very latest city: the *OMNIPOLIS*; a phantom-city, this one, a METACITY, wiithout limits and without laws, the capital to end all capitals of a spectral world that nonetheless declares itself to be *AXIS MUNDI* – in other words, the omnicentre of nowhere.

We are living like peaceful old burghers at the very centre of a cataclysm all too easy to create. All the finest minds, the most ingenious, are working out the most amazing ways to paint the word DESTRUCTION in the most ferocious images. It is not soldiers we should worry about. It is the ones who are fiddling with the fragile fuse that will set off the catastrophe, without really knowing

Pierre Mac Orlan went on to claim, seven years after Franz Kafka disappeared.

But his warning was swiftly elaborated:

The forces of panic can smash all the dykes of science. They behave like wild animals when a sign, read in the skies by the learned elephant of the tribe, causes the herd to flee in one direction to supposedly protective assumptions. Animals and men, when faced with fear, merge in the same ingenuity.[13]

And so, we have seen the emergence of a third anthropological type over the twentieth century: the exterminator. Not so much that butcher of a terrorism that has turned suicidal, the looming shadow of the lost soldier of the wars of days gone by; more the kind of butcher who ingeniously offers the means of putting an end to the world and to its *embedded* humanity – every possible means, including economic, technical and scientific – all the while being intimately persuaded of bringing Progress, a superior civilization...

In the light of this fatal downhill slide, we can better understand the imminent approaching of the transpolitical, that political gothic now busy taking over from the social gothic of the years that followed the First World War to which Alfred Döblin and countless film makers, in particular, bore witness.

Fear is, indeed, the essential element of the gothic. The great devastating wars have accordingly fed it without let up, from Verdun to Stalingrad, from Auschwitz to Hiroshima; and so has *the balance of terror* that has led to these first rumblings of *world civil war* we have registered in disbelief since the year 2001.

Between the mysteriously guarded machine for blowing up the Earth and the mindnumbing bombing raids that could take us back to the original mists, there is room for plenty of disastrous possibilities. In truth, we are circling a property whose inventory is not perhaps complete, but which we know is limited.

Written in 1942, this extract from *L'Avenir fantastique* (*The Fantastic Future*), by Pierre Mac Orlan, signals the end of fantastic socialism and the rise of a *revelation* that will bring the age of political revolutions to a close.

To take my turn at illustrating this circling of the property of a humanity now left once and for all with nothing to do, let me point out the latest ambitions of the moguls of speculation, those masters of the multinationals that are themselves weightlessly cut off from the real world of political economics, at home on a sixth continent, this one virtual.

Since the end of the twentieth century, outer space seems to be exerting a singular fascination over multi-millionaires. In May 1996, for example, the New Spirit of St Louis organization launched the 'X Prize,' designed to reward the first private firm capable of sending three people into suborbital flight above the globe and to repeat the exploit a fortnight later. Over twenty teams are in the running, including the team of Burt Rutan, the aviation designer responsible for *Voyager*, the first plane to have completed a round-the-world trip without stopping.

The aim of the prize, which is dedicated to the memory of Charles Lindbergh, is apparently to offer ordinary passengers

> a rocket flight into the black sky above the earth's atmosphere, [so they can] enjoy a few minutes of weightless excitement, then feel the thunderous deceleration of the aerodynamic drag on entry … a few minutes unencumbered by weight with an unobstructed view of the blue-fringed terrestrial orb and blackest night in plain daylight.[14]

Unveiled in April 2003, in the Mohave desert of California, Burt Rutan's registered entry seems to be the most advanced of the lot with its curious composite of spaceship, the rocket plane *SpaceShipOne*, and piloted turbojet carrier aircraft, *White Knight*, which launches it, ferrying it up to an altitude of fifteen kilometres, before this last stage, the rocket plane with its a hybrid rocket engine fuelled by nitrous oxide (laughing gas...), stabs through Earth's atmosphere and attains 100 kilometres altitude.

When it is running out of its 'funny' propellent, the high-flying object is supposed to coast along on its ballistic course, offering passengers over three minutes' suspension in weightless conditions.

They say the man financing this bizarre project is none other than Paul Allen, co-founder of Microsoft.

Is this yet another extreme sport (extremely costly in any case)? Or is it a clinical symptom of an outbreak of the mass psychosis of the besieged that has already struck the elite as a prelude to the building panic of the teeming hordes of this foreclosed old world?

Whatever the case may be, the meet for the launch was scheduled for December 17, 2003, a date that marks the one hundredth anniversary of the first flight of the Wright Brothers on the beach at Kitty Hawk... For the launch of a *flight into impasse,* the *cul-de-sac* of an adventure that is as pointless, in the end, as bungy jumping but that comes with a price tag of ten million dollars.

Notes

1. *Le Figaro,* 'Economie' supplement, December 5, 2002.
2. Cf. Luminet, J.-P., *Le Feu du ciel,* Paris: Le Cherche Midi, 2003.
3. *Le Monde,* June 28, 2002.
4. *Urbanisme,* special issue devoted to the 'private city,' 1998.
5. Falguières, P., *Les Chambres des merveilles,* Paris: Bayard, 2003.
6. Mauriès, P., *Les Cabinets de curiosités,* Paris: Gallimard, 2002.
7. Conrad, J., 'Karain: A Memory,' in *Tales of Unrest,* in *Selected Short Stories,* Ware: Wordsworth Classics, 1997, p. 50.
8. Virilio, P., *Polar Inertia: Theory, Culture & Society,* London: Sage Publications, 1999, translated by Patrick Camiller
9. Mac Orlan, P., 'La Bouteille à la mer,' in *L'Avenir fantastique* (no pagination).
10. Cf. Virilio, P., *The Information Bomb,* London: Verso, 2000, translated by Chris Turner.
11. Agamben, G., *Etat d'exception,* Paris: Editions du Seuil, 2003.
12. Mac Orlan, *op. cit.*
13. *ibid.*

14. Morin, H., 'Des multimillionnaires veulent faire lancer leurs propres engins spatiaux,' in *Le Monde*, May 10, 2003.

5

City of Panic

'When fear takes hold of me, I make up an image,' wrote Goethe. No need to make up such mental imagery these days. The instrumental image is instantly provided for us by television. Relating the in-flight explosion of the space shuttle, *Columbia,* one journalist observed: 'As though only repetition could remedy the inexplicable, *the image loop has become the signature of contemporary disasters.*' And so, the incessant round of satellites doing the vast ring road of the City-World is now doubled with the *looping* of terrorizing images in a 'state of siege' of the viewer's mind. The most obvious result is this raging mass psychosis of the BESIEGED affecting people throughout the world in the age of globalization.

For want of some *disaster writing* easily comprehensible to everyone, mass telecommunication tools are imposing their *signature* on us in a bid to identify terror.

'All our emotions and fears have been taken hostage since September 11,' Susan Sarandon pointed out appropriately. And it is no accident if, once again, it is the actresses and actors of America who have been the first to sniff out the building dangers, in a tradition including bygone actors such as Charlie Chaplin or John Garfield, both victims of McCarthyism.

Without any critical distance in the face of such a tidal wave, the viewer is thus now subject, not to the reproduction of the stereotyped pictures Walter Benjamin talked to us about, but to the collective hallucination of *a single image*, the optical theatre of a revolving terrorist panorama. What I propose to call the iconoclasm of PRESENTATION *in real time* now outdoes by a long shot the old iconoclasm of RE-PRESENTATION *in real space* of painted or sculpted images. The destruction of the Buddhas of Bamian in Afghanistan or the looting of the National Museum of Iraq in Baghdad are amongst the latest examples of such an iconoclasm.

This panic symptom of a veritable *loopng of the imaginary*, the SIEGE PSYCHOSIS that is today smiting people's minds, is the first sign typical of a FORECLOSURE that is temporal – and, let's hope, temporary – in this experiment, this life-size TEST, of globalization. It is the 'great retreat' of 'meta-geophysical' information that has become globe-spanning. In other words, what certain gurus are calling the *global brain,* a cybernetic vision that belongs to the political gothic that has taken over where the social gothic of the creepy 1930s left off.

If fear is the basic ingredient of the gothic, then the management of public fear, which kicked off some forty years ago with 'the balance of terror,' is back on active duty since the northern autumn of 2001 and right up to 'Operation Shock and Awe' in Iraq, where we witnessed a real multimedia 'magic show' as suicide bombers and coalition forces both had a tremendous time enthralling the hordes with a welter of pyrotechnical tricks. And although these stopped short of using those famous 'weapons of mass destruction,' they did involve using and abusing the equally massive 'weapons of mass communication,' whose arsenal never stops growing thanks to satellite dishes and the feats of 'psychological operations' (PSY OPS) designed to sow panic while pretending to quell it.

'The illusion of being a hyperpower stems from the demise of the Soviet Union,' according to Emmanuel Todd.[1] This optical illusion has lasted, it would seem, due to the lack of any declared enemy, on the one hand and, on the other, to the vanishing not only of Bin Laden and for a time Saddam Hussein, but also, and especially, to the unfindability of those 'weapons of mass destruction' that provided an excuse for triggering the American war of prevention.

It all looks a lot like a bunch of tricks from out of the prestidigitator's bag...

The United States are no better or worse than their opponents, Emmanual Todd continues and he concludes that: 'The Americans are doomed to go in for theatrical militarism vis-a-vis weak countries like Iraq and the Arab countries in general.'

How can we fail to register the justness of these words when we look at the 'theatre of operations' in the Near and Middle East or consider the bluffing involved in this wild escapade in the biblical desert?

In the north of Iraq, for instance, they bombed Mosul, not far from the ramparts of Ninevah. In the south, there was fighting around Karbala, a stone's throw from Babylon and the ruins of the 'tower to end all towers,' the tower of Babel... All this in the name of revenge for the collapse of the Twin Towers. Finallly, after the spiriting away of Saddam Hussein in full view of the famous 'Republican Guard,' the assault on Baghdad ended in the demolition of his statue in Fardus Square, televised live and in a loop, before the eyes of the whole world while, more discreetly, off-camera, the sack of Sumerian marvels was in train.

Apropos the 'decapitation operation' perpetrated on the effigy of Saddam Hussein, here's the account of one of the foreign correspondants present in the Iraqi capital at the time: 'It was the Americans who knocked it over to start with. At two in the afternoon, there were only about twenty Iraqis in the square. Two hours later, after a lot of rallying by loud-speaker, there were about a hundred – *just enough for the television pictures.*'[2]

So much for the mounting of the set. But, to thoroughly confirm just how far this 'political gothic' crafted for the crowd can go, listen to what happened next: 'The Hotel Palestine turned into a kind of theatre. From the balcony, you could see scenes being set up expressly for us,' Caroline Sitz, of French television channel, France 3, explained, her conclusion being: 'You never did see pictures of the battle of Baghdad, in any case.'

For want of such war pictures or pictures of the collateral damage caused by some 30,000 bombs dropped by the Coalition forces, and in the absence of a DISASTER MUSEUM that might alert us to the ravages of political recklessness, the 'information war' ended, in Iraq, in chaos with the capital delivered up to vandals and, as a bonus, the terrible spectacle of the MUSEUM DISASTER...

There is one other aspect, and not the least, to this sorry saga the fallout from which will probably be felt for several generations, and that is the fact that the name of ABRAHAM, the father of the faithful, a patriarch and native of Ur, to the north of Bassora, was on everyone's minds from beginning to end in this *trompe-l'œil crusade.*

While the tanks that charged into the desert storms bore the name of ABRAMS, the *postwar* declaration of President George W. Bush on May 1, 2003 was made off the coast of San Diego on board an aircraft carrier. The name of this vessel: *USS ABRAHAM LINCOLN*. For the apostles of a strategic tele-evangelism, this was a sign from the heavens, a sign that would fool only the faithful.

NEW YORK after the fall of the World Trade Center, BAGHDAD after the fall of Saddam Hussein, JERUSALEM and its 'dividing wall,' but equally HONG KONG or BEIJING, where village people in the vicinity of the city barricaded their hamlets in a bid to seal off the threat of atypical pneumonia... So many names on a list of urban agglomerations that could go on and on indefinitely.

CITIES OF PANIC that signal, more clearly than all the theories about urban chaos, the fact that *the greatest catastrophe of the twentieth century has been the city*, the contemporary metropolis of the disasters of Progress.

This is the real 'accident museum,' this megalopolis that takes itself for the navel, the *omphalos* of a final-ized humanity; this METACITY that no longer really takes *place*, since it now refuses to be located here or there the way the geopolitical capital of nations once used perfectly well to be.

90

The 'metapolitical' bubble of globalization is in fact gearing up to burst in turn and when it does so, it will free up a multitude of critical spaces ravaged by internal dissension in a worldwide civil war incommensurable with the local wars of days gone by.

Financial bubble, property bubble, bubble of the new technologies of information (or image) and communication (NTIC) that were especially good at communicating devastation and disaster. So many repeat burstings that signal, prematurely, the bursting of the 'geopolitical bubble of Europe,' thanks to its ill-considered expansion. But especially, and more seriously, the bursting of the *meta-geophysical bubble* of so-called globalization. Virtual settlement of a pseudo 'sixth continent' in weightless conditions whose *cybernetic virtues* are driving humanity to locking up its ideals of truth and liberty.

Whence this epidemic of siege psychosis currently contaminating the minds of the *loft society*, where the fractal revelation puts social revolution in the shade and where, with the aid of a little privatization, *critical space* overrules the public space of laws and the limits of the law.[3]

After the 'velvet revolution' in Czechoslovakia, we now have *velvet dislocation*, to say nothing of ethnic cleansing and its repeat ravages.

The proliferation of states that are weaker and weaker, soap bubble that bursts as it expands outwards and shrinks inwards. By way of example, we might cite the farcical declaration of that buffoon, Silvio Berlusconi, on the occasion of his accession to the presidency of the European Community on July 1, 2003: 'The frontiers of Europe need to push outwards to include Turkey, the Ukraine, Belarus and the Russian Federation.'

DECENTRALIZATION of government bodies sure looks good when the centre is nowhere and the circumference everywhere at once!

Since nothing is ever really WHOLE, fractalization is the way to go for all attempts at globalization. Actually, fracture and fragmentation are both induced by pressure or, more precisely, by compression of what claims to be 'complete' or, more to the point, 'completed'... Whence the EXCLUSION that marks the fatal culmination of all FORECLOSURE, once totalitarian, soon globalitarian.

Yet the implosion of the Soviet Union ought to have alerted us citizens of Old Europe that the sudden debacle of the satellite countries would not be without effect on the common destiny of Eurpeans!

As for the United States, those illusory victors of the 'Cold War' will bear the brunt of the fall of geo-strategic landmarks of the balance of terror, with the *terrorist imbalance* that now threatens the fate of humanity as a whole, here as well as there, that is, everywhere at once.

Finally, following the disintegration of the great geopoitical blocks, the time of the decline of the nation-state is with us, along with the beginnings of a strategic withdrawal to the metropolises.

This metropolarization is every bit as illusory bringing us, as it does, to the resurgence of the city-state, of which North America provides us with a perfect example, with its thirty million plus people cloistered in their private communities, on the pretext of social insecurity...

The same thing is happening in the Latin American sub-continent, at Sao Paulo, Bogota and Rio de Janeiro where gangs ravage the cities... Of course, in other places the ravaging is being done by 'paramilitary' or 'armed forces' that tout themselves as 'revolutionary' ... though they are more especially *revelationary* of the total chaos blighting the old 'right of citizenship.' Such chaos reinforces the sense of an urgent need for an enclosure or some remote camp and, ultimately, for a *police state* where 'the forces of law and order' would be privatized just as all public enterprises have been privatized, one after the other: transport, energy, postal services and telecommunications, and shortly, for the process is already well under way: *national armies.*

As an American soldier recently found himself able to retort goodnaturedly to an Iraqi worried about civilian insecurity in Baghdad after the liberation of Iraq: 'Don't worry, it's worse in Washington!'

93

'*The future city will thus be merely the solemn expansion of a torture chamber,*' Pierre Mac Orlan announced, already, in 1924.[4]

Present in Karachi for ten years, the Pakistani army recently pulled out, having failed to re-establish any semblance of order in a city where *twenty-three clandestine torture rooms,* controlled by local gangs, were discovered in 1992.

In this case, it's no longer the police who don't dare intervene in certain 'sensitive zones.' Now we have the army beating a retreat out of town.

The criminality of the various mafias is now topped by that of the innumerable urban gangs where the solitary crime is systematically doubled by the *crime as a social get-together in a closed milieu* – illegal confinement, gang bangs, torture – CAMP CRIMES that reproduce, on a smaller scale, those of the gulags and 'death camps,' where concentration of whole populations preceded their extermination. This brand of torture is 'civilian,' though that does not seem to bother those who, rightly, denounce the abominations of 'military' torture in Serbia or Algeria or elsewhere...

Confronted by this 'atrocity bazar' that our show-biz society refuses to censure, another kind of craziness, just as terrible, is making itself felt: in Dubai, in the Persian Gulf, the Emirates authorities have just launched a project baptized *THE WORLD*. What this involves is an archipelago composed of 250 artificial islands in the image of a map of the world – only, surrounded by a sophisticated protective barrier.

The construction of this estate is said to require hauling in twenty-five million tonnes of rock and some 200 million cubic metres of sand. The cost of this deluxe gulag: a mere 1.8 billion dollars.

FORECLOSURE, EXCLUSION... Megalopolitan hyperconcentration is now topped not only with mass hyperterrorism, but also a panicky delinquency that is dragging the human race back to the original dance of death. The city once more becomes a citadel, in other words, a target for all terrors, domestic or strategic.

At this point we should give the weight it deserves to the warning letter sent recently by twenty-seven Israeli pilots to their command:

> We, pilots in retirement and active pilots, are opposed to the illegal and immoral attacks of the kind that Israel has been launching in the settlements... We refuse to participate in air raids against civilian population centres. We refuse to continue to harm innocent civilians.[5]

After Guernica and Coventry, Hamburg and Dresden, not to mention Hiroshima and Nagasaki, it is in Jerusalem that aviators have dared, for the very first time, to denounce the *anti-city strategy* of which built-up areas have been the victims for nearly a century. And let's have no more claptrap here about disinherited urban wastelands, for it is all cities, their centres as much as their outskirts, that have never ceased being martyrized for the whole of the past hundred years.

Phosphorus bombs and napalm bombs, exploding time bombs for killing rescuers searching among ruins, atomic bombs and, more recently, *graphite blackout bombs* designed to provoke a great *blackout* of a city plunged into outer darkness as Belgrade was in May, 1999...

For a hundred years, all cities have been the target of firestorms that owe nothing to the *god of the armies* of Israel, but more prosaically to the Luftwaffe and its 'Condor Legion' in Spain, to the Royal Air Force and the US Air Force of Air Marshall Harris, chief designer of the strategic bombing campaigns in Germany. We might recall here biblical names for such terror raids – 'SODOM AND GOMORRAH,' for instance.

It is in the city and nowhere else that the WAR ON CIVILIANS was tested in the twentieth century, and this new war gradually took over from war involving a military field of honour.

After all, all the great battles of the past were always referred to by the name of some country field where they took place, from the Catalaunic fields of northern France to the plain of Waterloo (the French 'campagne' meaning both countryside and campaign)... The pitched battles of bygone empires' regiments *de Ligne* made way last century for the great strategic muddle of a characteristic form of destruction of urban centres similar to the 'open field' of the massacre of the prepolitical origins of history.

Since the concept of a 'war of zero deaths' applies only to helmeted troops of professionals, Clausewitz is ripe for packing away in the Invalides. His doctrine of war as the 'continuation of politics by other means' is now thoroughly outmoded... Outmoded by the 'imbalance of terror' – in other words, by the hyperpowerfulness of weapons of mass destruction able to extinguish all life on the planet.

But here, we might note in passing, the term 'extinguish' should be taken in its strictest sense, since the latest weapons systems are designed to function *as a network* and no longer only through radioactive radiation or through viral or microbial contamination, but further through the accident of a widespread breakdown in the power supply, one example amongst others of the hyperfragility of the technological progress of our societies.

Without going back too far, we might note, for example, the power failure that affected Cairo and the main towns of Egypt in 1990, occasioning indescribable chaos throughout the country.

In 1998, close to half the population of the Philippines, which is 35 million people, no longer had power available to them.

On January 2, 2001, it was the turn of northern India, where the 200 million or so inhabitants were suddenly deprived of electricity following a power failure at the Uttar Pradesh power station.

Lastly, on August 14, 2003, the North-East of the United States, specifically New York and Philadelphia, was struck by the biggest power outage ever seen in America, prompting the urgent shutdown of seven nuclear power plants.

We should add Rome, the 'Eternal City,' and the whole of Italy to this ominous list, with fifty-eight million inhabitants being deprived of power on September 28, 2003.

Yet listen to the bizarre commentary of the city fathers in charge of the New York municipality: 'Unlike with the power cut of 1965, there was no panic. No doubt this is one of the benign effects of 9/11.' There's that life-size test again... You just can't get away from this endless testing of the public emotion displayed by the teeming hordes![6]

Right after the Second World War, the American economist, John Kenneth Galbraith, studied the effects on the economy of the Reich of the panic felt by the civilian populations of Germany who had been bombed. Similarly, you can now analyse, *at home* rather than *over on enemy turf*, the dose of terror metropolitan masses can withstand.

How far can this go? How long can such contempt, such depraved indifference, in the face of *the torture chamber of the cities*, go on?

Another aspect of this distancing from, and habituation to, the *crime against humanity* constituted by the firestorms raining down in all impunity on civilian populations for the past century is the development of a new kind of adventure tourism: 'war tourism.' This brand of tourism sees travel agents organizing charter flights to the sites of bloody clashes in Israel and Palestine and elsewhere – in Latin America, for example, where Favela Tours and Exotic Tours run trips to the shanty towns of Rio de Janeiro and Sao Paulo.[7]

As the publicity for one of the tours says: 'Brazilians don't like visiting the favelas; foreigners, on the other hand, are curious, excited and sometimes a little tense, because they think something might happen to them.'

Following in the footsteps of extreme sports, the 'tourism of desolation' provides an adventure that is a product of this itinerant voyeurism that so cleverly completes the sedentary exhibitionism of television and its repeat atrocities.

Argentina has recently taken its turn as a most attractive destination for European and American tourists. The latest craze consists in zipping off to Buenos Aires to gawp at the aftermath of the collapse of the neo-liberal experiment of the 1990s.

As one journalist puts it: 'Visitors are gobsmacked *seeing so close-up* the violent contrasts of one of the most unequal countries on the planet.'[8]

One day, if we want to fight against panic, any kind of panic, we'll have to go beyond an urban ecology by reverting to some form of *geophysical politics*; a politics of matter and not just of light and its so-called 'escape velocity.'

If we don't, we will go through the wall of 'post-modern' wailing towards the wall of extermination. Not the end of the world, but its fatal FORECLOSURE, thus releasing a frightening temporal pressure analogous to the pressure of the ocean depths where only a few, totally blind, species survive.

To do this, we need a political economics of speed and its ACCELERATION that would parallel the political economics of wealth and its ACCUMULATION. On that score, let's hear it from the President of the Association of Private French Enterprises:

The crisis in the United States over the past two years has shown that *the Americans have lost their sense of measure as well as their sense of duration.* Everything hinges on knowing what time frames we're talking about here. When you see them trying to impose FAIR VALUE as a norm in accounting standards, meaning the market value at any given moment, you can only take fright and do all you can to resist the idea. Business needs time to grow and its value can't be reduced to the value of the market at a given moment.

Warren Buffett, the second richest man in America, agrees. On the new Internet technology bubble, he had this to say: 'That bubble was by far the biggest collective hallucination I've ever seen'... Whence all the legitimate suspicion about the so-called analysts of Wall Street and elsewhere.

In fact, in high finance as in foreign affairs, what we have seen in the past few years is not an acceleration of history that was supposed to lead to its premature end, but an *acceleration of reality*; a panic-driven phenomenon that has successively shattered the geostrategic givens of business as well as of the armed forces and has led to a farcical METAGEO-PHYSICAL politics of which the Iraqi conflict is a perfect example.

And so, for the whole of the last decade of the second millennium, instantaneous FORECLOS-URE found itself supplemented by EXCLUSION, a durable exclusion that is in the process of spreading far and wide. Immigration flows are a good indicator of this, announcing as they do the bursting of the globalization bubble.

Lastly, the temporal compression of interactive telecommunication has largely foreshadowed the mis-deameanours of a spatial and demographic saturation of our metropolitian agglomerations, which certain urbanists have been busily denouncing.[9]

Sorry Malthus, but no! Geophysical space is not insufficient for humanity. It is time, the *metageophysical space-time* of transport and instantaneous broadcasting, that has become illusory, in its mad hankering for extra-terrestrial liberation into a world that is virtual, the 'sixth continent.' And the obsessional nature of this idée fixe does not seem to worry anyone but the teeming masses. Those scientists who are such dab hands at trashing diversity aren't turning a hair, despite the fact that such trashing leads to a prison-like inertia, this POLAR INERTIA that acceleration of the real will fatally trigger one day, in the near future or soon after. But, after all, that is the very essence of *transpolitical gothic* – a world frozen in the monopoly of its finiteness!

'The Earth is a great big planet that goes in the sky covered in madmen,' Fontenelle observed, well over 200 years ago. Since then, the PHILOFOLLY of the mighty has not ceased, alas, to reduce the planet to nothing... To nothing, that is to say, to a few atrophied cities that pride themselves on being the epicentre of the world when they are merely lost citadels – in other words, targets, for firestorms! Since the beginning of the third millennium, the geostrategic space in which the defence and law of nations evolved has, in fact, swiftly shrunk. A researcher at the Hudson Institute in Washington puts it this way: 'America is at the head of an empire, but this group is a LIBERAL empire, not a territorial one.'

That exactly defines the 'critical space' of so-called economic globalization: escape velocity has wiped out the territory that was once the basis of *the legitimate state*, and the world of business, like the world of war, has found itself ever since suspended in weightless conditions, in the anguished wait for the great accident, this GLOBAL CRASH that won't fail to occur one of these days.

On the theme of the insularity of the New World, here's Benjamin Barber:

> How easy it was, *encircled by two oceans* and reinforced lately in its belief in sovereign invincibility by the novel utopia of a missile shield – technology construed *as a virtual ocean to protect us* from the world's turmoil and dangers – to persist in the illusion of sovereignty... Then came September 11 ... the myth of our independence can no longer be sustained.[10]

There you have it, the source of the metageophysics that dares to suggest that the territorial is not liberal and that the abolition of limits is the salvation of the people of the world!

For nearly a century, the peninsula of the Americas has extended right up to the firmament, like those 'skyscrapers' that are, in the end, merely elevated islands of a *skyline* that now circles the planet.

But the internal enemy of this 'above ground holiday resort' is obviously the terrorist activity of the transnational criminal organizations (TCOs) that are turning the geostrategy of the United States on its head.

Indeed, when no one has a home any more, when we are all, as they say, outsourced, it will be the world that becomes entirely terrorizing – something the crisis in the major airline companies is already fore-shadowing, here and there.

If the BUILDING is a vertical impasse, the foreign politics of NATION BUILDING is every bit as much. It is a 'no through road,' a fact the US Democrats are beginning to realize. Here is one of them, Senator Bob Graham of Florida, a candidate for the White House in 2004 (and co-chair of the House-Senate inquiry into the intelligence community's failures, set up following September 11):

The war against Iraq was a distraction. It has turned our attention away from the war on terrorism that we were lined up to win – we had al Qaeda on the ropes! Now the fight is slipping away from us. Intelligence existed and the government and special services knew about it, but it wasn't taken into account before 9/11. The same type of intelligence exists today and we're still doing nothing about it.

The term 'distraction' is exactly the word most appropriate to describe this 'theatrical militarism' referred to previously whereby the United States struts around bragging shamelessly while the world implodes in silence, or as good as...

One of the symptoms of this *outrageous bluster* is the sending to Iraq of the National Guard of Florida, two months after the official end of hostilities, in a bid to re-establish order in Baghdad.

Specialized in combating the aftermath of natural disasters, this unit – for whom this is, note, the first mission outside the United States – seems just as much at ease in the suburbs of the Iraqi capital as in the slums of America, in the midst of a civilian population hell bent on looting and exploring every possible opportunity for violence of every stripe. Natural disasters such as earthquakes or bushfires like those that blazed in California in recent years, or 'artificial' disasters such as an out-of-control *preventive war*: everything is now joining forces, it would seem, to jumble order and disorder, reality

105

and fiction, since 'civil peace' is no more guaranteed now by the law than the state of peace between nations is guaranteed by international organizations, starting with that flagship, the UN... In this sense, mass terrorism is a powerful revealer of the sudden globalization of chaos.

Conscious of the strategic impasse, certain Pentagon policy makers are preparing to retool the American military machine along the lines of some futurist model of ANTI-CHAOS ARMY.

Taking up the declaration of General Richard B. Myers, army chief and chairman of the joint chiefs of staff, who reckoned that 'war can't serve as a remedy for humanity's ills,' they hope, *a contrario*, to adapt certain 'army corps' to remedy the chaos of the modern postwar. Such armies will incorporate, this time officially, the role that today devolves to the National Guard of Florida in Iraq.

One of the most passionate supporters of the re-tooling idea is, moreover, General John Jumper, United States air force chief of staff, who helped craft the intensive air strikes over Afghanistan in the Afghanistan mission. Jumper is a man who no longer tries to conceal the necessity of mastering the ground, with the air force working closely with ground forces as Battlefield Airmen, thereby controlling the socio-political damage that results from a strategy too exclusively dependent on air and space power – too AIR-ORBITAL.

According to this model, the ANTI-ARMY chaos of anonymous and deterritorialized hyperterrorism would be superceded by the American invention of a powerful ANTI-PANIC ARMY that would expand the principle of *national defence* to cover *civil defence*.

This would be a huge program, creating a 'hyper-police,' in which the issue of the *state of exception* would be posed on a worldwide scale. Arthur Cebrowski, the director of the new US Department of Defense Office of Force Transformation, based in the Pentagon, is an avowed advocate of such a programme, as is clear from his denunciation of the perfectly anachronistic side of the *security policies* pursued by the major powers, policies that, he claims, 'tend to cut off the army from the planetary globalization under way.'[11]

To better understand the scope of this permutation, we need to go back a dozen years to the historic riots in Los Angeles, which ravaged the City of Angels on April 30, 1992, ending in a billion dollars' worth of damage and the death of about fifty people over three days.

At the time, it was to the troops of the US Army, fresh home from the first Gulf War, that the heavy task of intervening was entrusted, alongside the National Guard, to put an end to this metropolitan civil war in which communities clashed violently following the Rodney King scandal.

Today, in Baghdad, the reverse is happening because it is the National Guard of Florida that is called upon as reinforcements in support of the US Army in its desperate bid to re-establish order in the Iraqi capital now delivered up to all kinds of violence since the blitzkrieg when coalition tanks literally swept away the Iraqi state, public service, police and, more especially, the whole of the armed forces – some 400,000 trained personnel.

'Freedom is untidy. Free people are free to make mistakes and commit crimes and do bad things. We couldn't know how it would turn out,' declared Donald Rumsfeld, cynically, in the *New York Times* of May 18, 2003.

Disappearance of weapons of mass destruction, disappearance of Saddam Hussein following Bin Laden's disappearing act... But, especially, dispersal of the 'balance of terror' between nations rendered so very fragile... No doubt about it, the third millennium is kicking off with a bunch of magic tricks, vanishing acts on demand, a DISTRACTION, a bout of showbiz that has diverted attention away from chaos that is obviously here to stay, with the emergence of an endemic terrorist imbalance that must soon damage the international order patiently put in place last century. It will also equally damage that civil peace that is the basis of all democracy. And this return of the tragic will take our over-advanced societies from the EXOCOLONIZATION of the territorial empire of the past to the ENDOCOLONIZATION of a terminal empire currently in the works. Current migration movements already give some idea of the scope of the panic involved.

World that is closed, forclosed, in which we will all be OUTSOURCED, in other words, EXCLUDED from multipolar internationality and liberated into the extraterritoriality of a virtual and *unipolar* world.

Lately, in every business report and financial bulletin, one word keeps popping up like a *leitmotiv* and that word is PERIMETER. Expressions like 'constant perimeter' or 'funding perimeter' designate the whole set of subsidiaries that are taken into account in a firm's financial results.

The 'perimeter' has therefore become cardinal in assessing how healthy an enterprise is and its 'construction' these days obeys precise rules. For instance, if a bank's data processing is outsourced to an external consultancy service, it is 'outside the perimeter.'

Defining a business's perimeter can also serve to mask any cooking of the books, as in the Enron affair, in which dubious subsidiaries did not belong inside the famous perimeter, but did in fact hide from view losses that finally precipitated the dramatic fall of the gigantic American concern.

Expatriation thus has the dire consequence of *out-sourcing* not only low-cost production, but especially 'information' and therefore its *truth-reality*... Since we now know that everything that gets done with the use of computers is threatened with expatriation 'outside the perimeter,' it's not too hard to imagine what will happen next!

As a MEDEF (Mouvements des entreprises de France) initiative, the Observatoire de l'externaliza-tion, or Outsourcing Institute, has recently been set up, incrediby enough. According to the words of its president, its mission will be 'to convert as many businesses as possible' to the new practice that consists of entrusting the whole of a function or service to an *external* provider.[12] There was even a fair, held in Paris, from October 1 to 3, 2003. The title of the fair was, precisely, OUTSOURCING, that portmanteau buzzword that can now open any door, including the lid of Pandora's box.

Perhaps this is what they mean when they talk about an 'open society' – like the city offering itself without resistance to its invaders?

Whatever the case may be, the reversal of per-spective, denounced throughout these chapters, is manifest: the firm is no longer *introverted*, rooted in whatever specific 'locality,' but thoroughly *extraverted*, emancipated from all geophysical location, offered up to the chaos of a terminal neocolonial empire that is turning life on its head, for from now on: ELSEWHERE BEGINS HERE.

Notes

1. Emmanuel Todd on the subject of his book, *Après l'Empire*, Paris: Gallimard, 2002.
2. Amadou, F.,'La Couverture du conflit irakien a frustré les journalistes,' in *Le Monde*, May 21, 2003.
3. Cf. Virilio, P., *L'Espace critique*, Paris: Christian Bourgois, 1984.
4. This prophetic sentence on the part of the author of *Quai des brumes* dates from a time 10 years or so before the construction of the 'death camps' based on the model of the colonies thrown up under colonization of the East: *Ostcolonization*.
5. 'Protestation de vingt-sept pilotes israéliens,' Reuters – Agence France Presse, autumn, 2003.
6. On this point, see the Internet, 'The Dawn of the E-Bomb' by Michael Abrams, in which he talks not only about the 'information bomb' but also the 'electric bomb' (*Spectrum Online*, November 3, 2002).
7. Hiba, J., 'Le Brésil, ses plages et ses favelas,' in *Sud-Ouest*, November 7, 2003.

8. *Ibid.*

9. On this point, see Virilio, P. and Parent, CV., *Architecture principe 1966 et 1996,* Paris: Edition de L'Imprimeur, 1996, in particular the text by Paul Virilio, 'Manhattan out' (1966).

10. Barber, B. R., 'Beyond *Jihad vs McWorld*' in *The Nation,* January 21, 2002.

11. Isnard, J., 'Le Pentagone rêve d'une armée anti-chaos,' in *Le Monde,* May 2003. Cf. Paul Virilio, 'De la géopolitique à la métropolitique' in *La Ville et la Guerre,* Paris: Edition de L'Imprimeur, 1996.

12. Rollot, C., 'Le Medef promeut l'externalisation,' in *Le Monde,* November 7, 2002.

6

The Twilight of Place

Places die like people do even though they seem to subsist.

Joubert

The desert is subsistence. The desert is coincidence between the beginning and the end.

In the desert, destruction does not so much mean the decomposition of fertile soil or the salinity of the soil, as a gradual reduction in the dimensions making up the GEOSPHERE, this 'life size' of the mineral and vegetal elements of the star that bears us.

Actually, the slow miniaturization of our terrestrial habitat's proportions, through constant acceleration of all paths, is an insidious form of the *desertification of the world*. One generally perceived as 'progress,' at once techncial and political, which will bring people together, join distant cultures, by reducing distances and time gaps to nothing, or as good as...

This strange paradox of a happy and beneficial IN-CARCERATION makes no sense unless it deliberately puts us to work ginnying up for the 'extra-terrestrial' exodus of humanity, that great leap into the void of celestial nothingness: thanks, first, to aeronautics and, last, to astronautics.

If *escape velocity* effectively spells the world's old age, this is because the world itself must pass,[1] be lost forever, in promotion of a horizonless and limitless macrocosm where we will be alone, alone at last, having rammed two kinds of antagonistic desert end to end: the desert of *fullness* and the desert of the *vastness* of the cosmic void.

Already, the deliberate erosion of the platform of the AUTODROME, followed by the runway of the AERODROME, flagged this project of exile, in anticipation of the levelling of the launch sites of the COSMODROME.

The desert of the in-depth clearing of the terrestrial horizon foreshadows this crazily excessive *escape speed* that will shortly be able to exile us, definitively, from the human environment.

As the *plumb line* is the index of gravity, that is, of the fall of bodies, so the cleared horizon is the *level line* of the projection of bodies out of this world. On this subject, let's hear it from Ernst Jünger: 'A horizontal vertigo has been triggered inside me that incites me to run to the horizon, to roll there as far as the eye can see, just as the other vertigo incites me to fall.'[2]

From rolling as far as the eye can see to losing land altogether in flight or in astrophysical exodus: it is just one small step from one to the other or, more precisely, a quick launch from a LAUNCHING SITE.

In the end, the skyline is the apocalyptic sign of all deserts: *watery desert* of the sea, *earthy desert* of land, *airy desert* of the atmosphere that envelopes the planet and makes it habitable.

LITHOSPHERIC limit of caravans or HYDRO-SPHERIC limit of ships, the earthly horizon now extends to the zenith, right up to the extreme limit, this one ATMOSPHERIC, of the LIGHT GLOW that divides the rarified air of the stratosphere from the void where satellite and spaceship navigate; engines that all have an ARTIFICIAL HORIZON to guide their course, in addition to a gyroscope. Proof, if proof were needed, of the indispensible nature of *position markers, set coordinates* for vectors in movement: that ideal line or, more precisely, that *ideally deserted, infertile line.*

In this line drawn from one end of the planet to the other, all deserts are joined up, strung together, placed end to end, to signify 'departure' as well as 'arrival,' the ORTHODROMIC path, or GREAT CIRCLE trajectory, demonstrating the linear perfection of the shortest route from one point to another...

On this Earth, in the land of the living, the desert is thus merely a LINE, *the ridge line* of the earth's rotundity or the *shadow line* of its luminosity, this TERMINAL of day that produces Time: the local time of the history of humanity.

Dragged along by the rotation of the globe, the skyline never ceases fleeing. It leaps over the hills onto the plain and right up to the seaboard where it bounds over the limit of emerged lands. Here, *the desert is merely a race*, the headlong rush of the path of a celestial body moving within the universe. The 'desert of the full' is a voyage into the emptiness that life implies.

For the geophysicist, 'space is what prevents everything from being in the same place,' compressed within the density of a planet suspended over the abyss, and so the skyline is an expanding phenomenon, the silent memory of the parabolic origin of the world.

In fact, the horizon is the *littoral of appearances*: wherever the hydrosphere displays its oceanic curvature, the lithosphere exposes its heights. As for the atmosphere, to have any hope of perceiving its orbital limit, you need to acquire the propulsion power that propels the human breakout into space away from gravitational attraction.

And so, after twilight, that *shadowline* that separates day from night, the ultimate frontier between the desert of the full and the desert of the cosmic void surges up. This is the *twilight of places* where, one by one, all the markers of position and composition of apparent velocities disappear.

The desert of 'geophysical' fullness then bows out before the desert of a 'metageophysical' vastness that certain adventurers of the intellect still insist on calling 'astrophysical' despite the numerous uncertainties of astronomy.

And so the desert is, in the end, only the GROUND FLOOR of the measure of the world. There is no desertification without this LINE that stretches across the Earth as it does across the sky or over the surface of the water.

We should not forget, either, that 'acceleration arises in the opposite direction to Earth's gravity when a moving body gathers speed or when the direction of its movement changes.'[3] Whence the centrifugal and centripetal forces that knock us off course in our travels, our long-haul voyages.

The celestial body thus attracts us not only towards its centre. It attracts us equally towards the horizon of its periphery.

And so, if the world's axis attracts everything that *falls*, the horizon attracts everything that flees. The 'ground rush' of the parachutist, pulled towards impact with the ground, then becomes, for each and everyone of us, the 'life rush' of those marching towards their end.

'What will we be waiting for when we no longer need to wait in order to arrive?'[4] This is already an old question. In the year 2003, we could answer it by saying: *we will be waiting for the coming of what is left.*

This is not a paradox, although it sounds like one, for instantaneous telecommunications have now outstripped the speeds of transport and physical communications.

A *square horizon*, the traveller's screen has gradually but radically altered the *skyline* of travellers of old.

Encouraged by the immediacy of broadcasting, we are no longer waiting for anything more than the film's sequel in this global programme where the world puts itself on show through the intermediary of a monitor or, more precisely, a TERMINAL.

Suddenly, the *interface* of the cathode frame replaces the line of the *surface* of the ground and of the volume of the sky, of every ground and all the skies, from the extreme limit to the extreme proximity of the antipodes!

Let's suppose now that everything were not only *déjà vu* in this eery skylight but actually *déjà là* – already there – set up to stay within the media-generated hyperproximity of a spectral transparency, at once before our very eyes, yet still before us, *completely up against us.*

Like a fly against the windowpane or a fish in its glass bowl, we have reached the 'zero end point' where all distances cancel themselves out and where the intervals of space and time have disappeared, by turns, *in the desertification of the miniaturization of the world.*

If everything is there, already there, within reach, within earshot, then incarceration has achieved its apotheosis, confinement knows no bounds. Just as the deep-sea diver is acted on by water pressure, the viewer is subject to the enormous *temporal compression* of geophysical distances.

At that exact moment, the immobile traveller is subject not only to atmospheric pressure but also to the telescopic crushing of landscapes produced by those TELE-LENSES that have supplanted topographic limits.

Here, but where is that, in the end? The three dimensions are so tightly entangled they adapt themselves to exactly fit our senses. Like fabric, a skin-tight garment, the antipodes cover up the old perspectives.

No longer equipped with goggles but decked out in *the image suit of an expanse without expanse,* the network surfer is subject to the inertia of a celestial body that turns into a jacket, the *leotard* of his or her behaviours.

Moving forward in order to travel is no more necessary now than *moving back* the better to leap: the tête-à-tête now covers everything and the face-to-face is compulsory at every moment, since *voyeurism* and *exhibitionism* have become the same thing.

119

From now on, there is no more before, no more after, only 'during'... The space-time CONTINUUM is frozen in the cadaverous immobility of a sort of eternal present or, rather, in the *eternal presentation* of a voyage requiring no displacement, of an ON THE SPOT journey in which to go and to return have lost their giratory sense to co-exist, to coincide, in a *now* stripped of any *here.*

Having brought off the miniaturization of OBJECTS, machines, motors, technology has finally arrived at its ultimate ends in miniaturizing ITINER-ARIES, the confines of the world. In so doing, it achieves a new kind of 'pollution,' one that not only involves SUBSTANCES but equally DISTANCES... Length, breadth, height and depth lose their geo-metric significance and, instead, the flatness of *a relief without relief* shoots to the fore. In this flatness, the REAL-TIME perspective of the reception of signals wins out once and for all over the REAL-SPACE per-spective of the Quattrocentro.

Having reached this point, the 'vanishing point' of physical movement, REVERSIBILITY becomes the rule, *inside* and *outside* coincide, elsewhere as here!

Since arrival has completely taken over, it has be-come entirely pointless to leave. Since everything has already *reached its destination,* the relief of arrival no longer contrasts with the deep significance of departure.

Listen to that impenitent desert wanderer, Théodore Monod: 'There is nothing so apalling as to already see, from the spot you are about to leave, the spot you will reach that night or the next day, with nothing in between.'[5]

At such a moment, the desert of fullness is equalled only by its material density. The density of cancelled distances then takes over from the immensity of extended substances, from this geophysical rotundity that nonetheless contained our HABITAT.

From now on, the habitat of the animated being is scarcely more than a monk's HABIT, some habitable outfit intimately combining the outside and the inside.

Now decked out in 'simultaneous' climates rather than 'successive' ones like the seasons, the INSIDE is scarcely more than the satin lining of the OUTSIDE – only, of all 'outsides,' *from the skin to the antipodes*, perfectly fulfilling the prophecy of Paul Valéry when he said, as you'll recall: '*The deepest thing about man is his skin.*'

A skin or, more precisely, an osmotic membrane whose filter now contains all possible horizons: from the ocean threshhold to the vast Hercynian folds of geological expanses, not forgetting the architectonic reliefs of metropolitan agglomerations.

Not only has it become pointless to travel any great distance, to go over there, but also, and every bit as

121

much, *to turn back*, since *all surfaces are now face to face*; and the intensity of this presentation of appearances is equalled only by the inertia of the contemplator.

Decked out in the complete meterological array of the seasons, *planet-man* then drifts in the desert to end all deserts of the vastness of the void, desperately seeking not so much his like any more as the unlike, the foreign.

The telluric desert of CLAUSTROPHOBIA has been superceded by the desert of AGORAPHOBIA, this 'free fall' into the density of the temporal compression of the televisual horizon.

Where the old travel agent once declared: '*If you have the time, we have the space,*' the terminal of the video production room makes it clear that, in the absence of time, space-time itself is now lacking...

'*Time is only useful when it's not being used,*' as Oriental wisdom once had it. Can't we say the same thing, today, about space? After the pollution of NATURE, of the biodiversity of substances, aren't we heading for the imminent and definitive pollution of the LIFE-SIZE NATURE of distances, of an expanse that is more and more discredited in its vastness, its immensity?

'The Lord shall preserve thy going out and thy coming in from this time forth, and even for evermore.'[6] The desert is consistency, the desert is coincidence between birth and death. It is the place where all pretention is held in check.

In the desert, you become small, you become minimal. The telluric contraction of the earthquake is supplemented by the contrition of humility.

'I was everything and everything was nothing,' as the Stoic once put it... Here, the aesthetics of geophysical disappearance is backed by the ethics of the disappearance of all immoderation.

The loss of the life size caused by the speed of light in a vacuum – that final cosmological horizon – is now supplemented by the loss of the will to power.

The mirages of technology have outgunned those of desert space just as atmospheric lures have made way for the optical illusions of the special effects of the electromagnetic realm. From now on, '*you are wherever you cast your eyes*' (Paul Celan) and nowhere else.

Here, the inertia that undermines your corporeity also undermines the GLOBAL and the LOCAL; but also, just as much, the MOBILE and the IMMOBILE.

There are no words, there is no speech without silence, they say; and there is no voyage, no journey without distance. *Distance is the silence of the journey, of all journeys...* From here to there, from one to the other.

In the desert, silence is taken for granted: whether the mineral silence of the soil or the silence of the heavens, everything holds its peace – even for evermore.

123

The clean slate of a horizon that imposes the utmost destitution on the traveller, is further intensified by solitude, that absolute first step in the miniaturization of any being.

Indeed, how can we fail to see that, today, far from aggrandising the individual, progress in technology diminishes him, makes him smaller, to the point of shortly triggering his *physiological desertification* – which is another way of saying his emptiness, his uselessness.

Following the infantilism of the age of the machine, the age of the silence of the aborted will shortly be upon us, this awkward fœtus of the age of prosthetics. But to better grasp such a *reductionist* phenomenon we need to revert to the trinity of bodies that joins the trinity of persons.

There are three bodies: the desert is the face of the first, the TERRITORIAL BODY that sweeps humanity along in its cosmic course. The second is the SOCIAL BODY of the human race that engenders life. Lastly, there is the person who speaks, who willingly comes to life, the ANIMAL BODY of the person passing.

These are three distinct corporeities, certainly, but they would be nothing, or next to nothing, *without the energy that connects them, binds them, at the heart of the abyss of deep space.* Weightiness, weightlessness, universal attraction, GRAVITY is in fact a constituent of the REALITY of physical bodies, just as love and solidarity are constituents of the human race.

When we forget this, which is what we are now doing with the freeing up of the networks of the *virtual community*, we are subject to a GRAVITIONAL COLLAPSE, an unprecedented low that reaches the dimensions of each and every body: the *territorial body* is reduced to nothing, meaning to the time of the emission speed of waves; the *social body* gradually distintegrates in the concentration camps of the City; and, lastly, the *animal body* is rendered obsolete in its creative and procreative faculties by the progress of transgenic technologies.

So many impasses, desert-like *culs-de-sacs*. 'The distance between countries in a way makes up for the too great proximity in times,' Racine wrote some little time ago[7]... Such compensation has stopped working with the enormous temporal compression of globalization.

'I miss the World; I feel homesick for each and every country', cried Paul Morand, a victim of multiple solitude.

As for Chris Marker, the author of *Sans Soleil (Sunless)*, it's all over, he has done roaming the globe, it has lost its appeal: 'After a few round-the-world trips, the only thing that still interests me is banality. This perpetual coming and going is not some search for contrasts, it's a journey to the two extreme poles of survival.'[8]

But these disabused sentiments trumpeting the end of *exoticism* and the decline of the depth of field of appearances as of biodiversity, only imperfectly render the ultimate contraction that precedes the act of giving birth – a contraction of the HUMAN BODY itself, the desertification of *minimal man*.

To illustrate such an event, we need perhaps to begin with a tale about the latest kind of handicap or infirmity, one now afflicting the housebound invalid of these new times: 'His days generally begin at five o'clock, with a three to four kilometre run on a treadmill, while watching one of the many television channels he gets – MTV for music, SHOW TIME for movies or NICKLEODEON for kids' stuff.'[9]

Head honcho at Viacom, the seventy-five year-old Summer Redstone has made it: the end of his life resembles its beginning. *For him, the desert is a treadmill* where, as at the gym, an ON THE SPOT trek completes the stream of images. The race to the ends of the Earth has suddenly been overtaken by the speed of emission and reception of television channels where zapping reinvents the discovery of new continents.

In fact, technology has never stopped invading bodies: the *geophysical body* of territories rigged out for irrigation, with canals and wells and networks of bridges and roadways for traversing it in every direction, with Roman roads, royal roads, railway lines and highways – appropriate superstructures designed to control the environment of nations where autodromes and aerodromes were later the very first figures of a new DESERT OF SPEED. This is to say nothing of the stadium of Antiquity or of the 'closed circuit' of the hippodrome, figures emblematic of the *looping of high-speed journeys*, at the opposite extreme of the great population flows.

As for the 'City,' from its very beginnings, it has never ceased rigging out the *geopolitical body* of societies in order to discipline and toughen it up thanks to land registers and ramparts and the power of its economic and strategic productivity.

It remains for the third body to shortly be invaded: the *physical body* of our being. After the transport revolution of the nineteenth century and the transmission revolution of the twentieth, the bionic transplantation revolution is gearing up for the coming century.

Thanks to the miniaturization of nano-machines and electronic chips, BIOTECHNOLOGIES are going to be able to get into the very guts of the human animal, in order to stimulate or calm it down, to render it 'more competitive,' as they say. This will happen with the pacemaker, of course, but especially with the development of *electrostimulation,* in particular of man's lower limbs. Electrostimulation will soon *make paralytics walk,*[10] just as elsewhere the use of sensor captors will soon *make the blind see.*

At that point, all that will be left will be to bring off the end of all ends and *resurrect the dead*. Or as Karl Kraus put it: 'Amazement came to an end, the miracle grew!'[11]

'In the Mojave Desert, on the border between Nevada and California, there is a telephone box with broken windows and six bullet holes through it.'[12] Every day, a hundred calls stream in from the four corners of the globe, mostly without being answered...

'The property of Pacific Bell, the aluminium phone box has become the great model of the world over the last few years.'[13] It has become the focal point of the multiple solitude of this invisible community that peoples the limbos of virtual space.

Sometimes, as if by miracle, someone answers: 'I'm here.' And the unknown caller follows on with: 'It's great you're there, that you answered my call.'[14]

Dialogue of the deaf? Far from it. Dialogue of the blind or, more precisely, of the unseeing. *To go into the desert vocally* now rather than by following the trail, the royal road of the explorers, represents a strange metamorphosis, a sunless voyage of initiation, for speech that nonetheless remains speech because the sound perspective in this case blocks the visual perspective of the contemplative.

Like amateur radios but the opposite of the cameras of the WEB, those *livecams* that display *silent but live* images of a lost world, the pointless telephone of Pacific Bell offers us a glimpse of a world of poetic revelations about the scale of HYPERPROXIMITY in the age of the disappearance of the life size.

> Praised be You my Lord with all Your creatures, especially Sir Brother Sun,
> Who is the day through whom You give us light...
> Praised be You my Lord through our Sister, Mother Earth who sustains and governs us.

In the 'Canticle of All the Creatures,' Francis of Assisi, the saint stripped bare, sees the oddly close, great cosmic masses as so many campanions of his exile and his smallness.

In a premonition of the time of 'global machines,' Francisco divines the unheard-of possibility of a WORLD POETRY at the heart of the aridity of the cosmic desert. In his evangelical simplicity, *il Poverello* anticipates the day, not far off now, when *poverty will strike the elements themselves*, degrading not only vital substances but cosmic distances to boot.

At that precise moment, the denuded one warns us, creation and creatures will be *in unison*, stripped of everything, in the no place of a new sky and a new land.

Having become NOTHING, less than nothing, the GREAT EVERYTHING of cosmic appearances will make way for the COMPLETELY OTHER, for this common identity between the most vast and the most minute.

In the pain of a destitution that will be physical as much as geophysical, the astrophysical barreness will let us see the emotion behind a poetic issue *par excellence* – the issue of the intimate connection between MICROCOSM and MACROCOSM.

Apocalypse or Parousia? Incarceration or incarnation? 'Big Bang' or *'BIG CRUNCH'*?

Indeed, if *the desert grows, expands infinitely*, its growth is equalled only by that of a boundless belief, a confidence against all confidence that takes hold of the destitute one to the point where he can reverse the Stoic's phrase and confess: *'I am nothing – but that nothing is everything.'*

Desert of multiple solitude. Desert of the full, desert of the empty. Today HYBRIDIZATION has reached a peak; yet it introduces the issue of the anamorphosis of the geometric dimensions of a world endlessly speeded up.

If humility is simply the truth, the voice of the desert repeats in our ear: 'Whosoever measures themselves is nothing.'[15]

And so the twilight of places is every bit as much the twilight of the gods as the twilight of the plurality of worlds. Unison is not totalitarian unity but simply the parabolic threshold of CONNECTION as well as of PLACE – of mass, of energy, and of information;

and if HERE thereby has no more PLACE to be, this is because the miniaturization of the destitute has reached its end: not death, the end of all life, but the great life where he will be 'alone before the alone.'[16]

While end-of-millennium debates have raged, at the slightest provocation, over the catastrophic imminence of a WORLD ECONOMY deriving from the single market, the concrete possibility of a WORLD POETRY is seeing the light of day, equally, in the attraction of the desert of virtuality.

After incorporating the plants and minerals of the bucolic realm, and the rustic charm of wordly landscapes, and the sentimental episodes of the historic realm, depicted in legends and fables and sagas, contemporary poets are now turning, familiarly, to what still seemed not so long ago out of reach: the *black sun* of the missing mass, the torments of *black holes* or the gravitational mirages of celestial imagery.

INTIMISM is thereby no longer bound up with daily life so much as with the excesses of every stripe that science and technology these days generate.

'Mankind, look at yourself, you have in you the sky and the Earth,' the poet Hildegarde von Bingen divined, confirming, before Francis, the UNISON of measure and excess. She concluded that: 'Man is the enclosure of God's marvels.'[17]

Any man is thus not so much the centre of the world as the end of the world. Everywhere he passes or lingers, the desert spreads… Ronsard put it succinctly: 'Time does not pass, it is we who pass.'

It is we who ruin, one by one, the appearances of the world. Aging is merely the speed of the passage of the living and has been since the dawn of time! Shortly, and that's a promise, we will use up astrophysical space right down to the last cord, just as we have worn out geophysical space. Besides, besides, the famous THEORY OF COSMIC CORDS, like the theories of Newton and Einstein which it followed, is surely precisely a form of DENIAL OF INFINITY, the labourious knitting of a Penelope now bored waiting for the warrior's return.

'When you leave San Francisco on the way to Sacramento, a bit off Highway 80, you come to Rio Vista, which has 3,400 inhabitants. On the road that leads to the airport there, you'll also come across a certain Dennis M. Hope who has declared himself the biggest landowner in the world.' His land is over his head, on the moon.

The idea came to me at two o'clock in the morning some time in 1980. I'd been out of work for a year and in the middle of a divorce. I didn't have a dime. I said to myself that, if only I had some land, I could borrow money from the bank and set myself up in Los Angeles. At that moment, I looked up at the moon and I said to myself: there's plenty of virgin land up there![18]

Relying on an old rule of thumb from the buc-
caneer days of the Far West – first come, first served –
Hope declared himself owner of the moon. He later
also claimed ownership of Mars, followed by Venus,
and the rest of the solar system.

Illegal? The Outer Space Treaty, ratified in 1967,
does, effectively, prohibit appropriation of celestial
bodies. 'True,' our cosmic real estate trader of
Moonstates.com agrees. 'But the treaty only applies
to governments, not to private individuals.'[19]

At a point of convergence between world poetry
and the economy of the same name, Dennis M.
Hope is merely taking the logic of privatization to an
extreme: since everything is up for grabs, whether
islands, volcanoes or deserts – look at James Turrell's
RODEN CRATER, for example – the astrophysical
treaty of 1967 does not apply to lone individuals
as our moon merchant explains perfectly lucidly.
Wherever there is nothing and no one, all you have
to do is say the magic words, 'this is mine,' and the
miracle of celestial appropriation is accomplished.
For the lover of abysses, suffering from delusions of
grandeur, 'nothing is as vast as things that are empty,'
as Francis Bacon once said.

He who was alone, out of work and out of pocket
on the road to Sacramento, suddenly identified with
the celestial deserts of the night star.

'Watch out, he's a pauper!' Bernanos gave us fair
warning, already in 1933, about Chancellor Adolf

Hitler... The desert is not only the place of divine revelation of the Sinai. It is also the place of all super-human temptation, whether through the delirious delusions of science or those of the unconscious...

We should never forget that the desert inhabits the heart of the solitary man and that this 'inner desert' is the no place of all excess, the worst as much as the best.

Whether a star or disaster, in the end, with the exception of the blue planet, the desert is everywhere and Mars and Venus, along with the moon, are never more than *geospherical deserts;* the sum of a cosmic wasteland that anyone can hope to appropriate, any day, as so much uncultivated land for the development deal of a lifetime!

So, all that remains now is to put in place the ultimate voyage: the one that will bring the celestial bodies of astrophysics to the physical bodies of the species that bears life.

'To travel is above all to change your skin!' Antoine de Saint-Exupéry wrote.[20]

But that was just a metaphorical expression for the Aéropostale pilot. Today it has become a simple state-ment of the bleeding obvious: thanks to decryption of the human genome, the DNA helix will very soon allow access to vital appearances as well as *transgenic* exploration of the primordial seas, this *amniotic fluid* that is the exact opposite of the desert of cosmic deserts.

Thanks to the acceleration of computing speed, the *infinitely small* is about to open itself up to genetic discovery, as the *infinitely big* once did to the colonization of far-flung lands.

After the 1967 treaty prohibiting appropriation of celestial objects we will thus soon see a treaty that will prohibit privatization of the human genome.

And, indeed, on March 14 of the year 2000, Bill Clinton and Tony Blair issued a joint statement in which they asserted that: 'To realize full promise of the research, raw fundamental data on the human genome including the human DNA sequence and its variations, should be made freely available to scientists everywhere.' Freedom of information thereby no longer covers *public space* alone; it now takes on *genetic space*.

Beyond the 'political' treaties that are at the bottom of most border disputes between nations, this basically biopolitical declaration introduces the probability of future battles over the issue of modification of the living being, with cloning and hybridization being simply the logical outcome of eugenics.

To travel was still, not so long ago, *to change your skin*. It will soon be *to change your person* as you once changed your horse at the relay posts of the PONY EXPRESS!

Mail, correspondence *between people*, will no doubt be supplemented by correspondence *between genes*, the pairing of the best and fittest to survive to the detriment of the others, all the others.

Here, the desert will be the desert of the *series*, the desert of genetic perfection, the undivided reign of the perfect ones, the STANDARDIZATION OF LIFE.

The sequence of the human genome will then have replaced the photogram, that STANDARDIZATION OF VISION designed to control people's identity.

In the near future, and it's a promise, they reckon they'll be able to bring off *resurrection by replication*... The rocket stages necessary to attain sufficient velocity to escape the Earth, to get off the Rock, will be replaced by replication through successive cloning stages. This time, what will be attained, thanks to escape from the flesh, will be the outer limits of the solar system.

'Travel is a kind of door through which you leave reality behind to enter an unexplored reality that feels like a dream.' When Guy de Maupassant wrote those words, he could not have imagined he was anticipating the advent of the desert of the screen, of all screens. Compressed into the 'greenhouse effect' of a general acceleration, our contemporaries can't even imagine this disaster of perceptible appearances that nonetheless finishes off the job of the disaster of pollution and which goes by the name of: *virtual reality*.

Virtual reality is never more, in fact, than a *simulator of the loss of gravity* developed in experiments over the course of the twentieth century harnessing the weightlessness experienced during the first voyages of the astronauts.

Faced with the impossibility of simultaneously conducting both a long-haul voyage into a geophysical space miniaturized by supersonic speed and an astrophysical voyage beyond our solar system, we are falling back in the twenty-first century on an ERSATZ, a substitute reality: the *gravitationless reality* of a space that is now cybernetic. In doing so, we are opening the door to an unexplored reality that feels like a dream.

Desolation of a lost world, a scant general idea of which can be gleaned in all that is still provided by substantial ecology, because the loss not only of terrestrial distances but also of *concrete appearances* will make a veritable ECOLOGY OF IMAGES essential if we want to escape madness, serious alienation, in the near future and succeed in warding off the loss of the sense of reality.

In this OTHERWORLD, without contours and without continents, everything is possible. Created by the machine for other machines, 'this world is peopled by beings without skin or flesh, known as AVATARS.'[21]

For internauts at home in such improbable communities where role reversal is the norm, 'avatars are like a second skin. They are just images that float above the ground and can be moved around using a computer keyboard.'[22]

In the United States, giant 'avatar conferences' have already been held bringing together avatars from the four corners of the country – from places hundreds, if not thousands, of kilometres apart...

The desert is coexistence, the desert is coincidence between a being and his or her remote image.

The desert of sand and the desert of salt have been succeeded by the *desert of the senses.*

The sudden desertification of real presence has completed the degradation of material substances by pollution.

The drying up of the Aral Sea or the Baikal Lake is now topped by the flattening of the physiological relief of bodies.

From now on, *the desert of the screen* is expanding at the speed of the light of waves that propagate the ghosts of a desire that has not only become platonic but telescopic...

After the invention of the telescope and of tele-vision, this transgenic species is even set to innovate *tele-life* in which amorous frenzy will come down to a few grimaces and a handful of smileys...

Telescopy, endoscopy, fibroscopy... With the loss of physical contact, the screen of the TERMINAL pulverises the impact of emotions once shared.

As one habituée of this subtle network regrets: 'I don't have any friends in the virtual world, only in my real life.' As for lovers: 'To get yourself a cuddle, you stick your AVATAR right up against the other person's.'

Misery of a form of regression in which a return to playing with dolls is substituted for the great game of passion.

Like flies buzzing against a window, the internauts of this FORECLOSED world are all throwing themselves into a new sort of 'spell in the wilderness.' And that wilderness is only just beginning because the more the concrete world, the world of facts, shrinks, the more the abstract world of imaginary effects expands. Little by little the MIRAGE will take the place of the desert, of all the deserts: the desert of the full, of the star of life, or the desert of astronomical vacancy.

Stupefying narcotic products and their suggestive, mind-altering effects will be replaced by an *electronic product*, an hallucinogen that is likely once and for all to extinguish all discoveries and any amazement, in particular to do with perspective, that is, with the depth of field of perceptible appearances.

The classic perspectives of sight and hearing will be overlaid by the heretical persepective of touch, *touch at a distance.*

Already in Japan and the United States the process of broadcasting tactile sensations is getting off the ground.

With the interactivity of the TELE-TACT data glove offering *tactile feedback*, for instance, users can immerse themselves in a computer-generated world that reproduces the effects of trembling or vibrations or allows them to navigate around the most distant objects; not to mention the silhouette or profile of the person they are interacting with, which they can caress much the way a blind person would...

Curiously, the UNSEEING seems to be the obligatory reference or model for a number of interactive processes; as though audiovisual OVEREXPOSURE brought on an unknown form of blindness, the bedazzlement of general transparency provoking a PARAMNESIAC occultation of ordinary perception.

As for cybernetic telesexuality, there is no point going on because the exotic leisure industry is already running with it, especially in Japan.

But let's get back to the *desert of sensations*, to the life within the folds of some kind of software program, such as the SideWinder Force Feedback Wheel, by Microsoft:

This computer-game steering wheel features a custom-engineered force-feedback system connecting a powerful microprocessor to a miniaturised monitor that generates a force of 1,300 kg. A digital camera transmits the position of the wheel to the microprocessor; the monitor then creates the effects of force in order to simulate the utmost realism in driving: centrifugal force, engine vibrations, suspension or collision.[23]

So the 'flight simulator' is now joined by a *ground simulator,* simulating the gravitational deportation of the internaut, that armchair navigator who practices periscopic immersion in the desert of virtual reality.

At this stage, the *tactile perspective* could develop in such a way as to faciltate travelling to the most remote places in the not-too-distant future.

Following the steering wheel, the *feedback glove* will allow the virtual traveller to 'touch' objects and feel textures as a complement to image and sound.

We might even imagine that one day, having donned a suit of interactive data – THE DATA SUIT – our internaut will launch himself into a new kind of adventure tourism, discovering the ancient world with the assistance of positioning and surveillance satellites overflying him without letup.

As though playing a pinball machine, our explorer could then touch the summit of Everest or the slopes of Kilimanjaro with one single gesture... Sweep his hand over the shores of the Pacific, caress the wetness of the seas that lurk there... And, who knows? Maybe some day in the near future or soon after, he will TOUCH THE MOON, feel the aridity of the Sea of Tranquillity, searching somewhat gropingly for the tools dumped up there, in 1969, by the men of the *Apollo 11* mission.

At that instant, the *feedback straitjacket* of the inter-activity of the sense of touch will have totally interned us because the world as we know it and our own bodies will fit each other exactly.

PLANET MAN adrift in the cybernetic ether, the internaut will then experience the unbearable con-finement of his HABITAT, thanks to tele-contact with his HABIT, his gear.

Déjà vu, déjà là, within reach and within earshot, the blue planet will be no more than a cramped suburb, rendered not only insalubrious through its various forms of pollution, but further uninhabitable through its minuscule dimensions.

By hurling himself endlessly at the four cardinal points, *the earthling will soon find the Earth inhuman* – unhealthy.

Unless the reverse happens and inhuman trans-genic transhumanity finds the Earth decidedly *too down to earth!*

Then, the close of day, the twilight of a deserted planet, will be overtaken by night. The black night of an electromagnetic void where NUMBER takes over from NAME, from all names, and the *likely*, from the overwhelming advantage of its computing speed, will lord it over the *like*.

The convex desert of an expanding universe will be topped by the concave desert of the implosion of viewpoints.

An index of this sudden reversibility, the palindrome T.R.E.S.E.D may then stand in for the name of the D.E.S.E.R.T.[24]

Notes

1. 'For the fashion of this world passeth away': Saint Paul, I Corinthians 7: 31.
2. Ernst Jünger quoted in Gracq, J., *Carnets du grand chemin*, Paris: José Corti, 1992.
3. Jünger, E., *Le Contemplateur solitaire*, Paris: Grasset, 1975.
4. Virilio, P., *L'Insécurité du territoire*, Paris: Galilée, 1992.
5. Monod, T., *Méharées*, Arles: Actes Sud, 2001.
6. Psalm 121.
7. Jean Racine, second preface to *Bajazet*.
8. Marker, C., *Sans Soleil*, film, 1982.
9. Professional print media.
10. See the article on the demonstration by François Merger in Brussels in *Ouest-France*, March 21, 2000.
11. Kraus, K., 'Jugement dernier' (1918) in *Cette Grande Epoque*, Paris: Rivages. 2000.

12. Dubois, J.-P., 'Les appel du désert' in *Le Nouvel Observateur*, March 2, 2000.
13. *Ibid.*
14. *Ibid.*
15. Based loosely on David, *Psalms.*
16. *Les Sentences des pères du désert*, Paris: Editions de Solesmes, 1985, quoted by Davy, M.-M., *Le Désert intérieur*, Paris: Albin Michel, 1985.
17. Pernoud, R., *Hildegarde de Bingen*, Le Rocher: Paris: 1995, p. 102.
18. Gaudry, J.-B., 'Le Marchand de Lune californien' in *Ouest-France*, March 14, 2000.
19. *Ibid.*
20. Saint-Exupéry, Ā. de, *Oeuvres completes*, Paris: Gallimard, 1994, 'La bibliothèqe de la Pléiade' collection.
21. Arteta, S., 'Ma deuxième vie est virtuelle' in *Le Nouvel Observateur*, March 23, 2000.
22. *Ibid.*
23. Hai Nguyen, 'L'Interactivité tactile' in *Le Monde Interactif*, March 29, 2000.
24. In this instance, the palindrome is phonetic: Le Trait Cédé: the ceded trait or line, the line being the fading desert skyline that yields to the screen of the Virtual Desert.

Index

Abraham 16, 89, 90
Afghanistan 30, 41, 86, 100, 106
Ahmed, Gazi 35, 36
Allen, Paul – Microsoft and the
    X-Prize 82
Al Qaeda 92, 105
Aristotle 64
Association of Private French
    Enterprises 100–1
Auschwitz 29, 80
Avatars 137–9

Babel, Tower of 22, 43, 88
Babylon 19, 88
Bacon, Francis 133
Baghdad 15, 19, 43, 86, 88, 89, 90,
    93, 105, 108
Balkans 15, 52
Bamian, buddhas of 55
Barber, Benjamin 103
Bassora 89
Beaujon Hospital 4
Beijing 34, 90
Bellow, Saul 48
Benjamin, Walter 1, 2, 86

Berlin 1, 14, 38
Berlusconi, Silvio 92
Bernanos, Georges 133–4
Bin Laden, Osama 30, 87, 108
Bingen, Hildegard von 131–2
Bishop, Charles, 29
    the Tampa Affair 30
Blair, Tony 135
Bremer, Paul 19
Breton, André 47
Broch, Hermann 60
Buenos Aires 100
Buffett, Warren 101
Bush, George W. 16, 41, 67, 90

Caesar, Julius 15, 53
Cairo 97
Cebrowski, Arthur 107
Celan, Paul 123
Challenger 66
Chaplin, Charlie 86
Charyn, Jérôme 32
Chassin, Brigadier General 17
Chernobyl 27
China 5, 43, 67

Churchill, Winston 42
Cioran, Emile 53
Clausewitz 55, 97
Clinton, Bill 135
Colas, Francois 67
Columbia 66, 85
Commune of Paris 2
Concorde 27
Conrad, Joseph 69
Cosmic Cords 132
Coventry 95

Döblin, Alfred 89
Douhet, Guilio 14
Drancy 49
Dresden 14, 95
Dubai 94
Dubois, J.-P. 40
Duchamp, Marcel 48
Duras, Marguerite 48

Edwards, Dr Bradley 22
Enron 109
European Community 92
Expressionism 47

Ferry, Jules 12, 13
Firestorms, WWII 96
Foley, Thomas 36, 37
Fontenelle 102
Fortress America 68
Fressange, Inès de la 26

Galbraith, John Kenneth 98–9
Garfield, John 86
Goethe, Johann Wolfgang von 85
Gore, Al 59

Graham, Senator Bob 104–5
Great Wall of China 67
Ground Zero 14, 19
Guernica 95
Gulf War 16, 32, 44, 52, 60, 80, 122, 135

Halévy, Daniel 42
Hamas 36
Hamburg 95
Harris, Air Marshall 96
Harrison, Jim 77
Haussmann, Baron von 2, 12, 13, 14, 19
Hiroshima 14, 29, 42, 48, 80, 95
Hiroshima mon amour 48
Hitler, Adolf 4, 133–4
Hong Kong 90
Hope, Dennis M. 132–3
   The Outer Space Treaty 133
Hugo, Victor 3, 14, 22, 25, 30, 43
Human Genome Project 135
Hussein, Saddam 87, 88, 89, 90, 108

Impressionism 4, 9
IN SITU System 9–11
Iraq 15, 19, 35, 36, 37, 41, 42, 43, 77, 86, 87, 88, 93, 101, 104, 105, 106, 108

Jacob, Max 49
Jerusalem, and the dividing wall 90
John Paul II, Pope 42
Jomini, 53
Joubert, Joseph 113

Jumper, General John 106
Jünger, Ernst 114

Kafka, Franz 79
Karachi 94
Karbala 88
Klein, Naomi 38
Kraus, Karl 128
Kuala Lumpur 19

La Villette 4
Le Corbusier 18
Lindbergh, Charles 81
LINEAR project 67
Los Alamos 22
Los Angeles 107–8, 121, 133
Luftwaffe 96
Lyon 3

Mac Orlan, Pierre 72, 74–80, 94
Magritte, René 60
Malkovich, John 26
Malthus 102
Marker, Chris 125–6
Maupassant, Guy de 136
May '68 2
McChrystal, Major General Stanley 20
MEDEF 110
Mehring, Franz 11
Michaux, Henri 27
Michelet, Jules 15
Microsoft 82, 140–1
Monod, Théodore 121
Morand, Paul 125
Mosul 15, 88

Munich Games 54
Myers, General Richard B. 106

Nagasaki 14, 48, 95
Nantes 1, 3, 4
Napoleon 52, 53
NASA 66
Natef, David 39
National Guard of Florida 105–7
New York 18, 19, 21, 30, 48, 54, 90
Nietzche, Frederick 28
Ninevah 88
NTICs 58, 91
Nuremberg 38

Operation Peace in Galilee 35
Operation Shock and Awe 87
Otis, Elisha Graves 21
Outer Space Treaty 133

Pacific Bell 128–9
Paritsky, Yossef 35
Pascal 77
Pentagon 54, 107
Philadelphia, mayor of 15
    power failure 98
Philippines 98
Poe, Edgar Allan 26
Prague 6, 91
Pynchon, Thomas 27

Quarrel of the Iconoclasts 55

Racine, Jean 125
Raffarin, Jean-Pierre 34
RATP 10
Redstone, Summer 126

Resnais, Alain (*Hiroshima mon amour, Nuits et Brouillards*) 48
Rio de Janeiro 93, 99
Rome 98
Rommel, Marshall 53
Ronsard 132
Rumsfeld, Donald 108
Rutan, Burt, and the X-Prize 81

Sao Paulo 68, 93, 99
Saint-Exupéry, Antoine de 134
Saint Francis of Assisi 129
Sans Soleil 125–6
Sarandon, Susan 85
SARS 34, 90
Schweitzer, Albert 57
Shanghai 17
Sitz, Caroline 89
SpaceShipone, and the X-Prize 82
Stalingrad 51, 80
Star Wars 51, 67
Stockhausen, Karlheinz 29, 47, 48
Surrealism 47

Tampa 29, 30
TCOs 104

Thom, René 70
Titanic 28
Todd, Emmanuel 87, 88
Tokyo 21
Triolet, Elsa 14
Tunguska, and asteroid hit 66

Universal Exhibition 4, 12, 21
USS Abraham Lincoln 16, 90

Valéry, Paul 47, 77, 121
Viennese Actionism 57

Warhol, Andy 49, 60
Washington 30
    Hudson Institute 103
Waterloo 97
World Wide Fund for Nature and *Living Planet Report* 64, 65
Wright Brothers 82
WIC 18, 28, 29, 30, 54, 55, 80, 90

X-Prize 81, 82

Yokohama 21
Yves Saint Laurent 26